*I Will Be
Cleopatra*

I Will Be Cleopatra

An Actress's Journey

ZOE CALDWELL

W. W. Norton & Company
New York London

Copyright © 2001 by Zoe Caldwell

The name "The New York Public Library" is a registered mark and the property of The New York Public Library, Astor, Lenox and Tilden Foundations.

Frontispiece: Charles Laughton as Lear and Zoe Caldwell as Cordelia in *King Lear.* Shakespeare Memorial Theatre, Stratford-upon-Avon, 1959. Courtesy Shakespeare Memorial Theatre, Stratford-upon-Avon. Part One: Zoe Caldwell as a rosebud, 1937. Courtesy of Zoe Caldwell. Part Two: Zoe Caldwell as Helena and Dame Edith Evans as Countess of Rossillion. Shakespeare Memorial Theatre, Stratford-upon-Avon, 1959. Courtesy Shakespeare Memorial Theatre, Stratford-upon-Avon. Part Three: Christopher Plummer as Antony and Zoe Caldwell as Cleopatra. Festival Threatre, Stratford, Ontario, 1967. Photograph by Inger Morath, Courtesy of Stratford Festival of Canada. Photograph insert section: Pages 1–3: Courtesy of Zoe Caldwell; page 4: Shakespeare Memorial Theatre, Stratford-upon-Avon; pages 5–6: Photograph by Lewis Brown, Courtesy of the Minneapolis Theater Company; page 7: Courtesy of Stratford Festival of Canada; page 8: Courtesy of Don Lewis. Every effort has been made to contact all copyright holders. If proper acknowledgment has not been made, we ask that you contact our Permissions Department at 500 Fifth Avenue, New York, NY 10110.

All rights reserved
Printed in the United States of America
First published as a Norton paperback 2002

For information about permission to reproduce selections from this book, write to Permissions, W. W. Norton & Company, Inc., 500 Fifth Avenue, New York, NY 10110

The text of this book is composed in 11/15.5 Minion, with the display set in Minion Display Italic, Minion Display, and Europa Arabesque.
Composition by Tom Ernst.
Manufacturing by The Haddon Craftsmen, Inc.
Book design by Dana Sloan.
Production manager: Leelo Märjamaa-Reintal.

Library of Congress Cataloging-in-Publication Data

Caldwell, Zoe.
     I will be Cleopatra : an actress's journey / Zoe Caldwell.
          p.   cm.
     ISBN 0-393-04226-X
     1. Caldwell, Zoe. 2. Actors—Australia—Biography. I. Title.
PN2287.C235 A3 2001
792'.028'092—dc21
[B]   2001034510

ISBN 0-393-32360-9 pbk.

W. W. Norton & Company, Inc., 500 Fifth Avenue, New York, N.Y. 10110
www.wwnorton.com

W. W. Norton & Company Ltd., Castle House, 75/76 Wells Street, London W1T 3QT

1 2 3 4 5 6 7 8 9 0

To my beloved Robert

OTHER BOOKS IN
THE NORTON LECTURE SERIES

Book Business
by Jason Epstein

Savage Reprisals
by Peter Gay

Contents

PART III 1965–1967

I Will Be Cleopatra

Part One

1933–1957

~ 1 ~

I Am Born,
Who Am I?

I KNEW at a very early age that my job would be to stand in front of people, keeping them awake and in their seats, by telling other people's stories and using other people's words. I knew this because it was the only thing I could do. I sang, but not well enough, I danced, but not well enough, and because of my small motor skills disability, needlepoint and math were out of the question. So, keeping audiences awake and in their seats seemed the only way to go.

I was born on September 14, 1933, in Melbourne, Australia, which meant I was a Depression baby and Mum and Dad were on the dole—much to my father's shame. He had lost a successful plumbing business, but, as he used to say, in a depression you have to deal in things people need to survive and a leaky faucet could wait. He had become a bouncer at Percy Silk's Ballroom, not because he looked like a bouncer but because he had a way of saying "I think you've just worn out your welcome here, son" that seemed to strike fear into the hearts of hooligans and send them on their way, especially because he was always clad in black tie and a dinner jacket. Meanwhile, Mum, in her evening dress, took men onto the ballroom floor to dance the fox-trot, the Pride of Erin, and the Valeta waltz, for sixpence a set. Then she got pregnant. By Dad. They already had a twelve-year-old son, Bert, who worked before and after school, two jobs, delivering milk and newspapers. The money pooled was barely enough to feed three mouths. The promise of a fourth was not what the doctor ordered.

Mum's friends told her that she had no choice but to use the coat hanger, but Mum thought it might be fun to have me around, whoever I was, so she put her coat on the hanger and I was born. And a good thing too, because I seemed to bring them luck. Dad got a new job as a plumber and gas fitter at the Box Hill gasworks, the Depression began to recede, and Dad's Aunty Tilda, in Bolton, Lancashire, died and left him five hundred pounds.

Given her bequest, we left our terrace house in Moir Street, Glenferrie, and moved to a house in suburban Balwyn that was not attached to anybody. Five hundred pounds bought a lot in 1940. Dad bought a secondhand square maroon Willys and learned to drive, Mum got a carpet sweeper and carpets, Bert a secondhand bike and a screened-in sleepout, and I got my first bedroom. I was seven then and had been sleeping in a child's wooden crib in my parents' room. Of course, they slept in their marital bed and did the things done in a marital bed, while I felt how lucky they were to have a permanent sleep-over. All their lives, long after I had grown accustomed to sleeping in my own room, they slept in that bed and held on to each other.

But there was also in Moir Street a front room called, naturally, the "front room." It was tiny and had a few pieces of ugly furniture and our best linoleum. It was dusted once a week and the door was kept closed. Why that couldn't have been Bert's room, I'll never understand. Bert slept in a closet off the kitchen, which was meant to house our dishes and linen, but as we had so little of either, it seemed a waste of space and they made it into a tiny bedroom. Dad built shelves for books and Bert put hooks everywhere for clothes; there was a wooden box by his camp cot with a tiny lamp, and Mum made dark cotton curtains for some privacy. Bert, being twelve years older than me, never seemed like a sibling but more like a young dashing uncle.

So this was our family.

～ 2 ～

Moir Street

M Y FIRST memories are not of Balwyn, but of Moir Street. Our number was fifteen, but all the buildings were identical, adjoining terrace houses with iron railings and strange iron-lace-patterned fringe where the corrugated iron roof stopped. The iron had come from Europe as ballast in ships that then returned crammed with the hides of merino sheep from the outback. Because there seemed no practical use for all that fancy iron, it was used to decorate the houses. I'm glad it was, because without that strange decoration those little houses in Moir Street would have died of ugliness.

The front gate, I remember, opened to a patch of asphalt, three feet by six feet, then up two steps to the front door. Open the door and down a thin dark passage with the tiny front room on the right and Mum and Dad's small bedroom on the same side. The hall ended at the large kitchen with a one-fire black iron stove, which was always kept alight, even in summer. The lavatory, or "outhouse," was down at the bottom of the narrow garden where Dad grew gladiolas, dahlias, and vegetables. He also built a large cage where he kept his collection of vibrant colored and white cockatoos. These were a source of great pride, and no zoo ever had better-cared-for cockatoos. And then there were the dogs. If I had siblings, they were the dogs—mutts, strays, and endless puppies that, because of an overabundance, Dad would at times have to put into a potato sack and drown.

On Friday nights we all had a bath, one at a time, in a large tin tub in the kitchen, with water from the two black kettles on the stove. If you didn't get scalded, you definitely got clean. You see, we didn't need a bathroom, which was just as well because we didn't have one. The kitchen, with its large, well-scrubbed wooden table, was the hub of the house, as it is in my house today.

Attached to the back of the house and open to the garden was the washhouse, where the wash was boiled every Monday morning in a big copper cauldron. First, Mum and I, wearing pinnys, or aprons, scrubbed the dirty clothes and bed linen with brown Velvet soap on the washboard to get rid of the dirt and sweat. Then every-thing went into the "copper" with rather dainty squares of Reckitt's Blue, wrapped in cheesecloth and tied at the top, which made the water bright blue and the clothes so white you had to shade your eyes. I also remember that Reckitt's Blue was good for jellyfish stings, so we never left for the beach without a square of Reckitt's. When we did the laundry, the water was brought to a boil and stirred with a large bleached stick. After about half an hour the copper was emptied from the bottom and refilled with cold water. The wash was then stirred a bit more, taken out and put through the hand wringer, and pegged on the clothesline that ran down the garden, until the blessed fresh air dried it and we harvested it into a big basket.

Throughout the week, Mum would sit at the kitchen table, which was covered with an old blanket, and iron everything with flat irons from the stove. I know I sound old-fashioned, but there are certain rituals that unite women all over the world and washing is one of them. Today I have machines and chemicals to do my wash, which I still enjoy doing myself, but it just isn't the same. It never smells as sweet.

～ 3 ～

Mum

M Y MOTHER'S mother, Mary Hennerty, was a
large-boned, second-generation Irish-Catholic
Australian, born in Melbourne in 1872. I wish
I had known her. From what I was told, she was bright,
uneducated, with a marvelous humor, and read tea
leaves. But because she knew how desperate most of the
women were who came to her to know their future, she
kept quiet when really bad news showed at the bottom of
the cup.

When the local priest made a pass at her while she was
pregnant with her seventh child, she threw him down the
stairs and pulled all her children out of the Catholic
schools. Dad always said he married my mum because he
got on so well with his future mother-in-law. My grand-

mother was twenty when she met Francis Auguste Hivon. He had been born in 1867 in Mauritius, a British-ruled island off the east coast of Africa, and had come to Melbourne to make his fortune as a coach builder. Francis Hivon was a small, dark Frenchman with little humor but, as family history has it, a lot of sex. He quickly got my grandmother pregnant with my mother, and they settled into a life of poverty and twelve more kids.

Born in January 1896 and being the eldest of thirteen, my mother, named Zoe Viale Hivon, got very little schooling, yet she loved to write and write she did. It didn't help that she couldn't spell and had no comprehension of punctuation, but she was not a fool. She had seen books and realized that proper writing required capital letters every now and then, and symbols that looked like dots and hooks with more dots on the end and little dots with tails. So whenever she finished a piece of writing, she would, it seemed, take a jug of punctuation and pour it over the page. No one could understand what she was writing; it remained her secret, until I became old enough and schooled enough to puzzle out her meaning and push all those strange signs into their rightful places.

I am forever grateful to Mum for allowing me to correct her writing, because it taught me to follow the "score" of a playwright and quickly know what he or she wanted to let the audience know. When I act, direct, or teach, I act, direct, and teach punctuation.

I once had a student who was, as they used to say, a flagrant homosexual. He was a sweet young man and talented, but he could never come to rest. Whatever the part, he never was still and if he made a mistake he slapped his own face. He knew I liked him and he trusted me. One day in class I gave him *Hamlet* to read and asked him to do nothing with his body, just observe the punctuation, and if he were to make a mistake, he should slap *my* face. "To be or not to be" is read often by actors wishing to impose themselves upon the prince so that they will show you "their" Hamlet. I've learned that if you cease to think about yourself and concentrate on obeying the punctuation, the pressure is removed, and you will reveal yourself and be Hamlet; and because the body and soul are uniquely yours, you will be "your" Hamlet. It was not easy for this young man, but as he obeyed the discipline of the text he became younger, more vulnerable, and eventually pure male. He never slapped my face, for he made no mistakes.

While my mum was not educated, she had a beautiful singing voice and was a marvelous dancer with very pretty legs. I have my father's legs. When my mother was only fourteen, in 1910, she toured India, China, and Japan with the Bandmanners Company, which took Gilbert and Sullivan to the English populations stranded in that midday sun. The tour lasted a year and turned Mum into a virtual nun. That year she saw so much sex in the dressing rooms that she made a vow never to have anything to do with that immoral thing called "theatre." She never looked back. She went into a knitting factory. She had black eyes, loved life, had great innocence, but no humor.

Humor is, to me, the saving grace. The more serious the problem, the more the need for humor. Sometimes, when seeing a play, I think, if it had more humor it would be more profound.

Mum was perhaps most unusual in her total lack of self. She looked out of herself to other people and was never afraid to say what she felt. When I met Sir Malcolm Sargent, who had just conducted the London Philharmonic Orchestra, in Adelaide, he told me he had had the most marvelous compliment paid him by my mother. She had said that she knew he was a great conductor because when he conducted she heard not only the loud instruments but also the tiniest cymbal. We both laughed. Mum made you laugh but she didn't know why.

~ 4 ~

Dad

ALBERT Francis Caldwell, my dad's father, was a tall, thin, penny-pinching tea taster who was born in Bolton, Lancashire, on August 25, 1865. He was, of course, a Virgo. He was a good-looking man with dark eyes whose Methodist upbringing forbade him to drink, swear, dance, or go to the theatre, but didn't forbid him to don his purple smoking jacket and tasseled cap after dinner and fill the house with pipe smoke. I remember that image and, though I couldn't take my eyes off him, he filled me with fear. Whatever a tea taster was, I always imagined him sitting very straight in his purple outfit holding a perfect porcelain cup. He lived to the age of ninety-eight.

His wife, Grandma Caldwell, was tiny and adorable,

with bright blue eyes and a sharp tongue. Remarkable for her time, she was a third-generation Australian, born in a miner's tent at Yandoit on the goldfields, on March 3, 1870, which made her a glorious Pisces. Like her husband, she lived a long time and died when she was ninety-nine. Her only regret was that she couldn't receive the telegram from the Queen that all citizens of the British Commonwealth are sent on their one-hundredth birthday.

Her name was Fanny, and she was worried that Mum would name me after her. I think Fanny Caldwell would look swell on a marquee. Maybe *Medea* with Fanny Caldwell wouldn't work. I'd have to stick to comedy, but that has its advantages too.

Albert Edgar Caldwell, my dad, was not, however, Fanny's favorite child. He arrived ten months after her firstborn, Ada, too soon, too soon, and he was colicky. He was a rebel from the moment he felt he was not wanted. He rejected his strict religious upbringing. He did everything wrong. He swore, smoked, danced, and—as soon as he was old enough—wore oxblood boots, went out with wild women, and, even on Sunday, attended every performance in town. Vaudeville, opera, plays, musicals, ballet, circus, but he would not set foot in a Methodist church. Or any other church, unless for a wedding or a funeral. He felt, and did until the day he died, that theatre allowed all your senses full rein and church, as he knew it, reined them in.

Edgar, as he was called, was wounded in Egypt in the Great War, suffering a leg injury that never healed, and he was sent to England to be hospitalized. As soon as he was allowed a recuperation leave, he took a train to Bolton, his father's home town. My dad was five foot nine and a half, slim, reddish hair, blue eyes, and he was in uniform. Aunty Tilda in Bolton fell for her nephew and that's how we later received the five hundred pounds that changed our lives. Following that leave, he was returned to the western front and managed to survive until the armistice in November 1918, when he returned to Australia.

He then met Zoe Hivon, with her black eyes, full breasts, and pretty legs, and she, like Aunty Tilda, fell for him. She worked at the knitting factory with Dad's sister Ada, who talked about Zoe Hivon all the time—what she said, what she did, where she had been. Her life was so different from Ada's, but they became friends and eventually Ada asked Zoe to the Caldwells' small house in the country at Mount Evelyn for the weekend. Of course, Edgar was there. He taught Zoe to ride a horse, but she fell and broke her arm. Suddenly she needed to be taken care of. Mum was not one to take care of herself, so given the circumstances Dad was just the man to do it. Of course they fell in love. "Yours till hell freezes over—Edgar" was how he ended one love letter to her. How could she resist such a sweet talker?

Their courtship was a whirlwind of theatregoing. Dad made it clear that if Mum wanted him, she must also want the theatre, and after one year, they married. Dad, who had been such a wild rascal, became a really good husband. I once said to Mum, "Why doesn't Dad bring you flowers or chocolates as other dads bring their wives?"

"He doesn't need to, Zoe. He hasn't done anything."

They were total opposites and were happily married for fifty years.

We never went to the movies, or very rarely, but I saw every singer, dancer, actor, or vaudevillian who came to Melbourne. At this time, Bert was already eighteen and wasn't always with us, because the Second World War had begun and he was about to join the Army. Mum and I would take the tram to the city, go straight to the box office of whatever theatre we wanted, hoping to be first in line. Dad left work, cleaned up, put on a suit, and joined us. As soon as the box office opened, we bought our tickets, and raced up the stone steps to the top balcony—"the gods," as they were called, the cheapest seats. We sat front and center on the benches and had our thermos of tea and sandwiches. If the show was a hit, the "packers" would begin to push the person sitting on the aisle with their padded brooms, and everyone would bunch up closer until we were packed in tightly together. "Peanuts or lollies," the boys in the bellhop caps with their trays would cry out until the magical moment when the lights dimmed, the audience hushed, the orchestra having tuned up, begins to play and the extraordinary world of illusion began. I still have the same feeling of excitement today when the houselights dim down and it's all about to begin.

Then of course came the thrill of a player lifting his head high and looking at you. You, up there in the "gods"! I tend to do a lot of head-high acting—I guess in remembrance, because today the top balcony has largely gone out of style, except for opera. But not for me—never for me.

This early theatregoing made a huge impression, but so did a family who lived opposite us in Moir Street in a house, a real house. Their names were Mr. and Mrs. English and they had six children—Zillah, Joan, Phyllis, Nettie, Spider, and Macka. Zillah was fourteen years old when I was born and was always at our house asking Mum could she bathe me, feed me, dress me, or take me out in the pram. I was a sort of pet and the girls called me Judy. I don't know why, but they would dress me in their clothes, stand me on their kitchen table, and teach me songs and imitations of people like Mae West. Zillah and Joan even took me with them, in my pram, to Doris Gee's toe, tap, and ballet class. Soon I was learning the hula and singing "Lovely Hula Hands." That is how I was in my first dancing concert at two years and ten months, wearing a grass skirt and a lei and strumming a toy ukulele.

The English girls put my feet on the stage. Mum made lessons possible, but it was Albert Edgar who lit the fire and let me see the importance of theatre to life.

～ 5 ～

Balwyn

OUR MOVE to Balwyn, in 1940, was some sort of miracle, not because of the plot of land around each house or the Willys or the carpet sweeper or my bedroom but because of Winifred Moverly Browne, who taught elocution. She was a large breasted, imposing woman who was married to John Alexander Browne, a very fine singer. They were a civilized, childless couple in their fifties, living in Balwyn, and when Mum and I walked up the large flight of stone steps to their handsome house and knocked the knocker, our hearts were pounding.

You see, since I was three, Mum and Dad had seen to it that I was taught all the skills that I might need for my chosen job. Like Zillah and Joan English, I took toe, tap, and ballet from Doris Gee, who was a bit rough and smelled of creosote. Eurythmics and calisthenics from Vera Hopton, who was tall and elegant. Musical appreciation from Beverly Watts, a nice man. I had worked very hard at all of them and won many medals. But we knew nothing about elocution and here we were at the door of the best teacher in Melbourne, or so Beverly Watts said. It was Beverly who had told Mum I should learn elocution and as Mrs. Browne lived in Balwyn, why not see if she would take me?

Mrs. Browne opened the door and we were led into a dark house with comfortable chairs, one large grand piano, and books. I never dreamed there could be so many books in one place. Mrs. Browne gave us some lemonade, looked me over, asked me to breathe, put her hand on my diaphragm, and asked me to speak. "Anything," she said, "a song or a nursery rhyme." I sang a song. She would take me on spec, no charge, for six weeks, twice a week. At the end of those first six weeks Mrs. Browne said to Mum, "Don't worry about the money. She interests me. Let's go on with the work."

I don't know why Mrs. Browne made such a generous decision. I never asked her. Maybe because I was dressed so plainly and wore glasses. Maybe because she could see we were not well off. I knew I was bright but not special.

Whatever the reason, Mrs. Winifred Moverly Browne gave me my powerful diaphragm, a voice that can be heard, and a knowledge of Shakespeare that makes me able to speak it, understand it, and swim in it.

I suppose I became her surrogate daughter, and she had such knowledge to impart that finding a receptacle so open gave her joy. She took me to galleries and concerts and put books in my hands that would never have been there otherwise. I read all of Dickens, but no Proust. My parents, who exposed me to so much theatre, would have shown me this world too, had they known about it.

Although Mum loved having a daughter, she was not possessive and always let me go to other people: Mrs. Browne; the English family. While she kept an eye on me, I never felt possessed by her. She was not a "theatre mum."

Under Mrs. Browne's tutelage, I became a professional actress at the age of nine, playing "Slightly Soiled," one of the lost boys in *Peter Pan*. The production ran for the whole Christmas season, eight weeks at the Tivoli Theatre. When I now tell anyone that my first professional job was Slightly Soiled, at nine years old, they look sad for the abuse of such a young child. In fact, this is the name of the character in J. M. Barrie's play who arrives as a baby in Never-Never Land tied up in a bundle of laundry marked "Slightly Soiled."

Decades later, three days before Mrs. Browne died, I was in Melbourne and visited her in hospital. She was a tiny wisp of a woman then and I had taken her three bunches of violets, her favorite flower. I put them on her chest so she could smell them and a nurse came in, and in that dreadful voice people sometimes use to children and old people, said, "Ah, pet, we don't want those on your nice clean nightie, do we?"

"That is exactly where we do want them," I said quite fiercely.

Then I took this frail little person in my arms and rocked her gently. Life, death, old, young, powerful, powerless—it is such a mystery.

~ 6 ~

School

WHEN I was three years old, before our move to Balwyn, whooping cough left me with a weak muscle in my left eye—a "boss eye," as we say in Australia, which means you can keep one eye on your work and the other on the boss. Great for grownups but tough for kids. "Cross-eyed Caldwell" wore little wire-rimmed glasses to correct the condition. The Depression didn't help with a plague called infantile paralysis or poliomyelitis, which was highly contagious, especially in the poorer areas. There were, on our street, about fifteen kids who went to the local state school, and when we heard that they were dropping like flies, Mum decided that I was not to play with them and I wouldn't go to school with them.

This was, of course, the 1930s, long before the advent

of the Salk vaccine. Poliomyelitis could cripple you for life, so I was kept behind the bars of our iron fence and eventually sent to the Seventh-Day Adventist private school, where Mum believed polio was less frequent. Mum, always in her best coat, hat, and gloves, deposited and collected me there every day. Naturally, I didn't fit in anywhere. I longed to play in the street with the kids but that was forbidden. I also longed to be a vegetarian like the kids I went to school with, but we ate meat and Dad used the Lord's name in vain, so obviously I wasn't one of them. And things didn't improve when we moved to Balwyn.

I was enrolled in the Balwyn State School in 1940 and promptly got pneumonia. I had to wear thermagene wool vests under my clothes and woolen stockings. I must have looked a strange sight and the kids avoided me unless they wanted to punch someone. They knew I was the "someone" because I didn't punch back or cry. One day Mum came to collect me just as a girl named Lorraine punched me. Mum got very angry—with me, not with Lorraine. "Zoe, don't you ever let anyone do that to you again." The next day, when Lorraine started punching, I swung my leather school bag at her only to hear Mum say, "Zoe, stop that at once. How dare you hit that little girl." Honestly, if I didn't know what a glorious life I've had, I would weep for myself.

We were not a churchgoing family but we observed all the rituals—none of which made sense to me. What was all this talk of resurrection in the fall with everything dying? (In Australia, of course, Easter comes with autumn.)

I became very religious. Anglican Church twice a day on Sundays and sometimes a quick stopover on week-days. I took church and God seriously, and didn't want it just on Sundays with a new dress and a pretty hat. I *believed.* I wanted to know *why* I should believe. Like research for a part. The point at which all religions come together interests me, not where they separate and run to secret corners. For three years I tried to make it all belong and when it didn't, I stopped going to church. Maybe Dad was right about the theatre. . . .

When time came for my secondary school, Mum said, "Zoe, you are going to Methodist Ladies' College. And I've got a job at Holeproof stocking factory to pay for it." My mum was some woman.

I'd always heard that, when I was in my pram, she would walk me past a great gray building with a gray fortress wall and wrought-iron gates with a metal star and the initials MLC. Mum would say that someday I would be a student at that school and become a lady. I was now twelve and the time had come.

I once more put on the private school costume—gray

tunic, gray blazer with insignia on pocket, gray lyle stockings, gray blouse, gray felt hat, gray gloves, and black lace-up shoes. I threw away my glasses. Maybe this time I would fit in. But no. My dad was a plumber and my mum worked in a factory. Their dads were doctors, barristers, and members of Parliament, and their mothers didn't work.

What they didn't know was that I had that power to keep audiences awake and in their seats. Every day after school I had something other than homework, gossip, and boys. I had lessons, classes, and radio serials. An exciting young man by the name of Morris West was just beginning his career writing and directing radio serials set in the Australian outback. He heard that I read well for my age, so I became the young girl or boy in nearly all of his plays. Now I had another skill—radio. I began to understand how important the voice was and how subtle an instrument it was and how essential it was to observe the punctuation, to make the meaning clear. Audiences may not be so bright individually, but when they are together as a collective intelligence, they become very bright and are able to understand anything. The trick is to keep their intelligence engaged. If they know exactly what you're saying, they will follow you anywhere. Lose them for a minute and they may nod off and you will lose them for the entire time you are together. It is a rigorous mental business, acting. If the playwright is good, serve him or her and you will find a great load lifted from your shoulders. The playwright will make the audience laugh or cry, not you.

When I was twelve years old, because of my work in the radio serials I was given a half-hour news and interviews program, geared for children, for radio station 3DB. My co-host was another twelve year old, David Wittener, who went to Scotch College, the boys' equivalent to MLC. We went out to the Gellibrand Lighthouse in Port Phillip Bay, Melbourne's harbor, with our microphone and interviewed the lighthouse keeper. We went to a party at the Aquarium with twenty-four deaf and dumb children and tried to describe their joy. We interviewed J. W. Martin Sr., a diver employed by the Melbourne Harbour Trust, while he was at work ten fathoms below Victoria Dock. He spoke to us from inside his diver's suit and helmet. Each week we were given biographical material on a visiting celebrity. We wrote out the questions that we wanted the answers to, and since we were twelve, our questions were different than those asked by grownups. We were not of course to be rude but truly inquisitive, and our guests answered us truly. General Sir Thomas Blamey, commander in chief of the Australian Army, midshipman Charles Lutyens, grandson of the great English architect Sir Edwin Lutyens, and Wee Georgie Wood, an extraordinary vaudevillian who was a midget, were three of our guests. Every Monday I got to know a bit of the life of some special person and I learned that interviewing is preparation and listening, really listening.

Saturday nights were the nights I entertained—not gentleman callers, but guests at birthday parties, weddings, and Masonic lodge evenings. I was a stand-up storyteller. The Canadian Stephen Leacock had written my favorite stories, which were outrageously funny but also sad. John Alexander Browne, my elocution teacher's husband, was the singer, in white tie and tails, and I wore a silver lamé gown. I was fourteen years old. Again, I learned to listen but this time to the audience. They told me how far I could go. I still listen to the audience and am constantly amazed at how far they want me to go, but I must be the one in control. Laughter is good and necessary but if you can suddenly make an audience weep in the middle of a laugh, it's better. Although I can't remember how much, I was paid for all my work. Dad opened a bank account in my name and insisted I visit the bank once a week. He said, "You can put it in or take it out; just know you earned it and it's yours."

I actually liked MLC. I didn't rebel. I just went undercover and got reasonably good grades. History and English I devoured, never late for assembly, nice to everyone, didn't take speech or dramatic classes, but I did claim to have my period every week so as to be excused from sports, for which I had no love or ability. At least it worked until the school nurse asked me to come to her room for a serious talk.

There were of course teenage parties with the gramophone churning out "In The Mood" and fifteen-year-old boys from Scotch College shuffling you around and rubbing their pimples against your shoulder and trying to put their hands on your breasts, such as they were, and smelling of wax and thinking of sex. I was a good dancer. I was now fifteen, and had already willingly given my virginity to a terrific eighteen-year-old last maker, someone who built wooden molds for shoes. Given my vast experience, I sure didn't need the shuffling and the snuffling.

In the end, however, I did not graduate from the Methodist Ladies College. I suppose I had been spoiled. Mrs. Browne was like a private tutor, and in school I was pretending to learn in a room full of others. Frustrated, I finally just left.

The excitement I felt was enormous. At last I was free. Free to start. But start where? All local Melbourne theatre was amateur. Only the commercial management firms of J. C. Williamson and Garnet H. Carroll brought people from London and New York and surrounded them with good Australian actors. There were also two important amateur theatres, one run by Brett Randall (the Little Theatre) and the other by Frank Thring (the Arrow Theatre). I didn't know what to do. I had always been paid when I worked, but now, at seventeen, I had to become an amateur. I took some jobs teaching speech at Catholic schools for virtually nothing and learned to love nuns.

My image of nuns up to that time was of restricted women in medieval costumes with shaved heads, heavily under the rule of men, from the Pope down to that little priest who had been thrown downstairs by Grandma. I believed they didn't have a lot to laugh about. But what I found were spirited women who, when they weren't frightening the kids into submission, were thoughtful, inquisitive, and longing for laughter. They asked me questions about my life, and I asked them about theirs, and often the talk was on the verge of bawdy. I came to look forward to the lunch hour.

I still had my radio serials, so without being a burden on Mum and Dad, I was free to take any night job offered me. I was prepared, as any actor worth his salt should be, to play or understudy, make the tea or sweep the floors.

There must have been a great number of understudies, tea makers, and floor sweepers because I ended up playing parts. My first real part, in a real play, *The Gleam* by Warren Chetham-Strode, was that of a schoolgirl. I supplied my own costume. It was an ordinary English play but it taught me a lesson that has conditioned my whole life in the theatre. I had a few lines but mainly I had to listen— not act listening, but listen. As a solo performer, I had known that most of the oxygen was to be taken up by me, like being an only child. But now I had siblings, other actors, and my job was to take only the amount of oxygen that was rightfully mine or the part I was playing. That was a big lesson. Listen to the other characters and share the stage. I am now quite a good listener and the older I get, the more magical the sharing becomes (Ralph Richardson was the greatest listener I ever had the privilege of seeing, perhaps because he was the greatest actor I ever saw).

I believe that there is no better teacher than a paying audience. It was essential for me to be in a fully professional company all year-round, but that was not possible at that time. And God looked down. God is very good, if fully aware of the situation, in seeking out the right person to challenge and change a piece of the world that needs it. He knows the person must be young, virile, bullheaded, ambitious, and sufficiently neurotic. He chose John Sumner.

Sumner was an Englishman schooled from the age of eight in a choir school, which means he sang his way through his tuition all through England, Scotland, and even America. His father had died when he was fourteen and his idolized brother was shot down in the war in 1940. At sixteen John Sumner joined the Merchant Navy as a cadet and sailed the world. Australia fascinated him.

When the war ended, he became an assistant stage manager in repertory in the English provinces, was noticed for his intelligence and discipline, and was taken on board the great H. M. Tennent, Ltd., London's most important producing company, whose captain, Hugh (Binkie) Beaumont, was as good as they get. John quickly became stage manager of some very important productions in London's West End, working with Laurence Olivier, Vivien Leigh, Anthony Quayle, Terence Rattigan, and Athene Seyler, seeing how the best theatre was made and how much discipline it took. He had applied for a job as manager of a theatre in the heart of Melbourne University, one that was used for student productions, lectures, and the film society. Tyrone Guthrie had interviewed him in London by saying, "Why the hell do you want to go to Australia? You'll be on your own, no costume, lighting, wig or scenic department to ring for help."

"Because I believe that constant change is necessary in

the theatre and the stage is most alive when offering different plays and tackling different subjects all the time."

"All right, if you want to go to Australia—go," said Guthrie.

John then married the Honorable Karis Mond, a gorgeous, flaming ginger head, and together they set sail for Australia on board the Pacific and Orient's *Himalaya* in January 1952. Karis, I remember, was a great help to John and being "Honorable" didn't hurt because Australians love titles.

It didn't take John long to realize what was needed and he set about to make it happen—the first fully professional fortnightly repertory company in Australia, in Melbourne! He was only twenty-eight years old, a tall, perversely good-looking, dark-haired man with deep, dark eyes and a great skull.

He would eventually change the whole theatre landscape in Australia by putting his life in the service of enabling Australian actors to work full-time at their profession. England had repertory and touring companies. America had stock and touring companies. These places were where actors learned their craft. We had the odd chance of a tour in a commercial hit, but you can't train actors that way. John Sumner and his Honorable Karis made sure they saw whatever theatre there was in Melbourne and selected their company from what they saw. I was asked to an interview and invited to become an initial member of the Union Theatre Repertory Company. I would have to be ready to start in six months, and once we started, we would work year-round. Six months! I needed to earn some real money before I began.

~ 7 ~

Fowler's

I HAD MYSELF written out of the radio serials because sometimes I wasn't used for two or three months. After I quit teaching in the schools, I went to work at Fowler's pickle factory under an assumed name, Sue Vale. I realized that we were required to sign in when we punched the clock in the morning. I couldn't use my own name, which was already somewhat known in Melbourne, and with my small motor skills disability, a long name like Jeanette MacPherson might take me the whole day to write. So I became Sue Vale. Sue's husband had had an accident and that's why she needed to work. She put her hair in rollers, covered them with a scarf à la Carmen Miranda, and punched the clock at seven thirty, six mornings a week. My mother was furious. I was supposed to become a lady, not a factory worker pretending to be someone else. What Mum didn't understand was that this was my way of surviving. I loved the experience. I learned so much. I belonged at last and the girls were kind because of my husband's accident.

The heat, the smells, the sound of the machinery meant that all your senses were assaulted all the time but you were free to think—mainly about how good-looking the fellow on the tomato pulp was. But there was a freedom and I was playing a part that I seemed born to play until the forewoman, a fierce little lady with a tight permanent, and I had a knock-down-drag-out about the beetroot belt. The conveyor belts were designed to shuffle the boiling hot fruit and vegetables so they could be peeled, pitted, and made ready for bottles and tins. Fair enough. But the beetroot belt was the worst. Your clothes and hands were stained, sometimes for days, and there was nothing you could do about it. Sue Vale never complained, until one day she just walked away to the peach belt. Up came the forewoman.

"Over to the beetroot belt please!"

"No!" Sue said.

"All right then, start crown-sealing the tomato sauce bottles!"

I didn't know what that entailed so that's what I did. I

soon learned that the bottle of boiling tomato sauce jiggles its way along the belt. With your left hand, you place it on the crown-sealing machine, while with your right foot, you press the pedal that drops the metal cap on to the top of the bottle, sealing it. Then with your right hand, you take the bottle and put it on another belt. This process goes on all day, except for two tea breaks and a lunch break. It was remarkable and always made me laugh to see everyone in that huge place stop, as soon as the whistle blew, leaving the last bit of peel on the fruit, and run up the stairs to have their time off; all the girls with scarves around their hair suddenly stripped off their rubber gloves. The decibel level in the factory was high, but so was the level in our break room—filled with female voices gossiping and laughing.

At our first break that day, I said to one of the girls, "The pads of my hands are really burning."

"Stuff a hankie up your glove, love. What job are you on?"

"Crown-sealing the tomato sauce bottles."

"Oh, Shirl's old job? Poor Shirl."

"What do you mean, poor Shirl?" I sensed danger.

"One of the bottles exploded and did a real job on her face. But she got good compensation."

What did I think I was doing? Earning enough

money to see me through until I could start my life's job as an actress only to find I had no face? So I went straight to the forewoman and demanded to be taken off the crown-sealing or have protection for my face. Otherwise, I would leave. *Very loudly*, I said all this. What had happened? Where was the wimp?

"So leave," said the forewoman.

I took off my gloves, went upstairs to my locker for my toothbrush and towel, waved good-bye to the girls, and left. I was sad to leave them, but through Sue Vale, I realized I didn't have to be the one who got punched.

Mum was thrilled. Nonetheless, I still had four months to go before John Sumner's company started rehearsals, so I applied for a job as an usherette at the grandest of the first-run movie houses, the Regent Theatre, on the grandest street in Melbourne, Collins Street. It was and still is marvelously ornate with a grand staircase with dark red carpet leading to the foyer, which had lighted alcoves containing rich gilt vases full of rich gilt flowers. The doors that opened to the inside of the theatre, with its red velvet plush seats and dark golden walls, were manned by usherettes. They took your ticket and opened the door. You were then led by another usherette who pointed her flashlight to the floor for your comfort and then lifted it to show you to your seat. All usherettes wore a long maroon skirt with a white blouse and a nifty maroon jacket to the waist, a huge white lace handkerchief in the top pocket, and a gardenia in her hair. They spoke softly and were very polite. I saw *The Snows of Kilimanjaro* with Gregory Peck and Susan Hayward for two months and *Call Me Madam* with Ethel Merman enough times to marvel at her phrasing.

～ 8 ～

*The Union
Theatre Rep*

THE SIX months went by in a flash. With my face scrubbed clean of all makeup except the brown around my eyes and my freshly washed hair pulled into a tight ponytail, I set off for the great day, the first rehearsal of the Union Theatre Repertory Company. My entrance did not bode well, as I arrived ten minutes late—for the last time in my life. John Sumner gave me such a dressing-down and made everyone—front of house, backstage crew, costume department, the whole company—sit silently for ten minutes. Then he said, "Now we can begin." The silent humiliation was excruciating.

Today I arrive at the theatre three hours before curtain, which is a bit excessive, but it shows how well I learn.

There are many different forms of repertory. Weekly repertory, fortnightly repertory, and the big regional theatres where as many as three or four plays are rehearsed and fed into the season: the Royal Shakespeare Company; Stratford, Ontario; the National Theatre of Great Britain; and the Guthrie Theatre in Minneapolis are examples of this most important kind of repertory. The Vivian Beaumont, at Lincoln Center in New York, was built to be a repertory company. That is what Robert Whitehead, its original director, intended, but because of ignorance and pride on the part of the board, that dream was never fulfilled. Fortnightly rep means you open a play on Monday night. Tuesday morning you read the next play and start to rehearse, playing one play at night, rehearsing another during the day. After two weeks, on Sunday night you dress rehearse and open again on Monday. One year without a break—you have to be fit.

My life of after-school classes and work had been preparing me for this experience. I was not one day out of work for two years. All young actors should be so lucky. Every two weeks a new part, a different play, and John Sumner, who knew what he was doing, ruled. I never thought of his age. I just knew that he knew the way and I'd better follow. Never did any company member ask to play a particular role and there were no leading players.

You played what you were given no matter how large, no matter how small. You were a company member and served the company. That was your job. If you were sixty years too young for the part, you found out what it felt to be sixty years older. We performed every playwright, including Shakespeare, Shaw, Sheridan, Miller, Coward, Williams, although no Australian playwright. Once a season we did a revue with songs and dances and sketches. It was an Australian company with young talented actors and old talented actors and no one could pull rank. It could have made a marvelous country actually, everybody being used and important but not too important. It was, in fact, my country, my world. To go to work every day and earn your living doing what you know how to do is very powerful.

The men in the company were paid eleven pounds a week, the women ten. This was the early 1950s. I still lived at home, paid rent, and whenever a couch or lamp or chair or bed or a curtain was missing, it was because it was needed at the theatre, onstage. Dad often said he loved going to the Union Theatre to see his furniture.

At twenty, I was fully employed, doing what made me free. My dad had, at last, sold the Willys and bought a secondhand white Peugeot, which I drove too quickly and a little dangerously, but I'd been driving since I was sixteen and felt sure behind the wheel. By now, my brother was married with two kids. Mum was still working at Holeproof because it made her feel free to spend money on the house, Dad, the grandchildren, and herself—and suddenly I wanted a baby! I bought a very feminine maternity top and put a small pillow at my waist, and in my lunch break, went into the grand shops along Collins Street and looked at baby clothes. I knew I wasn't pregnant, but I had the strongest urge to have a baby. Maybe if I pretended and acted the part well enough, the longing would go away. I told Mum. Eventually Dad said, "Zoe, I hear you want a baby. Why not try a dog?"

"*A dog!!!*"

"Well not a dog," said Mum. "A brand-new puppy from a kennel and you will select it and buy it and get up in the night to feed it and walk it and train it and bathe it and neither your father nor I will have anything to do with it."

And that's what I did. And it wasn't easy because I was a working mother, but Thomas Seymour Mendip, a reddish gold, long-haired cocker spaniel, cured me of my maternal longing for a good ten years.

The Thomas Seymour was in honor of the Thomas in *The Young Elizabeth*, by Jennette Dowling and Francis Letton, and Thomas Mendip was in honor of the Thomas in Christopher Fry's *The Lady's Not for Burning*. I had played Elizabeth and was now preparing to play Jennet Jourdemayne, when someone gave me a 78 recording of the glorious John Gielgud/Pamela Brown/Richard Burton production. For the only time in my life, I decided to deny myself completely and simply imitate Pamela Brown, who was a wondrously sensual, important English actress in her middle thirties, with a voice the color of stout.

Well, you can imagine how dumb that was: my twenty-year-old body with Pamela Brown's voice—just the voice, I hadn't even seen her play it. Macabre really, and I was rightly and soundly trounced.

Actors, like painters, copy a little of the actors they admire until they become a composite of all they have chosen to be like and step out in their own skins, their own voices, and are themselves. That is why it is so important that there are many actors, different actors, for the young actor to see and copy and discard. That's what happens in life—same in the theatre.

When I first saw Alfred Lunt in *The Visit* in London in 1960, I was stunned to see a truly great actor use his eyes and hands in a gesture that was central to Laurence Olivier. Olivier used it in every part and young actors would imitate the gesture to sort of send him up. There was Lunt, a much older, great actor copying Larry. Then I heard that Laurence Olivier had toured with the Lunts when he was a very young actor, playing a small part.

The Union Theatre Rep's first season was, surprisingly, successful. We played fifteen plays in thirty-one weeks and began to attract a loyal audience, one that discovered that seeing the same actors playing different parts every two weeks brought a whole new dimension to their theatregoing. We had a week's vacation and then returned to rehearse for a tour of provincial towns in Victoria.

~ 9 ~

The Tour

OUR FIRST tour, under the auspices of the Council of Adult Education, consisted of one of the plays from the season, George Bernard Shaw's *Pygmalion*, being taken all over the state of Victoria for five months. I played Eliza, the cockney flower girl who becomes a lady, and I became, as was everyone else, a jack-of-all-trades.

We had a huge van for the sets, the costumes, the lighting equipment, and the big hampers that contained our makeup boxes and props. The company sat up front. We played two nights and one matinée in each town— Geelong, Warnambool, Cohuna, Bendigo, Wonthaggi, Korumburra, Wangaratta, Ballarat, Wodonga, Echuca, Patchewollock, up and down the Murray River. Real Ned

Kelly country. Five pubs, two churches, a town hall, and miles of bush between towns. Sheep, wallabies, and swagmen (itinerant workers), long dusty roads, and every now and then a small farm, or a large station with thousands of acres and large gum trees.

You drove into town, unloaded the van, cleaned and ironed the costumes, set up the dressing rooms, set the stage, did the show, went to the bunfight (town reception), socialized, changed the setup for the next day, and then dropped into whatever hotel bed you had been allotted. There was very little lovemaking; you simply didn't have the energy. There was very little fighting; I guess we didn't have the energy for that either.

Of course, for the second tour we did have Barry Humpheys, who was not yet a Dame but simply—and I might say purely, but I won't—"Mrs. Edna Everage from Humoresque Street, Moonee Ponds." He was wicked, smart as a whip, and infuriating. He was as thin as a pin with long dank hair and played Orsino in *Twelfth Night* in black velvet. Orsino is the romantic male lead and Viola is in love with him as soon as she sees him. But since she is disguised as a boy, she must conceal her love; to rub salt into the wound, she is sent as a messenger to the lady Olivia, who has Orsino's heart. On his first entrance, he got laughs—just by entering—and then one night his "If music be the food of love, play on" was followed by "Enough!" A very long pause, so off came the record. Then Orsino said, "No!—More!" And the poor stage manager had to throw the record back on the turntable, the needle back on the record, making the most godawful scratch, causing Orsino to say, "It's not so sweet now as it was before," making Barry's first Orsino scene a riot of laughs. It was tough to stand in the wings as Viola and adore him.

Barry also had a habit of pretending to be spastic while walking down a country street or having a cup of tea in a local café. He liked to watch how people reacted to someone in distress or at least different from themselves and to see what degree of pity he could evoke in them. He would go so far as to pour a little jug of milk on his head and his tea on mine. I was forever amazed at how sweet the waitresses were, the sympathetic care for Barry or looks to me, as if they knew how hard it was for me to be his sister. Sister! At this point I was not even his friend. I realize that there is a strong core of this provocation in his work today, so I guess he was studying too, and he graduated with top honors.

One day on the second tour when I was ironing the costumes in the wintry sun between two buildings, which had something to do with the town hall where we were to play that night, a roly-poly man, who walked as though he had just gotten off a ship, began to talk about his new play. He was our Feste, a poet, and my friend. He, like all of us, was an original member of the company but he sometimes directed. He had been born and brought up near the abattoirs in Melbourne. His family was large in number and in size. The brothers played football (Australian rules) and the sisters were pretty, laughed a lot, and had boyfriends. I knew Ray was different. He had had a bad burn on his hand when he was a child and had to spend a lot of time in hospital for skin grafts. This made him cherish his privacy so, whenever he came home for a bit, he set up a small corner, like a tent, with a sheet and a tiny lamp and read. No sports, no loud laughing, just reading and writing. He began to write plays. First about gods and goddesses, then about kings and queens, then lords and ladies, and then about rich Australian landowners (squatters) and their wives. All from his imagination.

By the mid-1950s, Ray Lawler was writing from his own bloodstream about the people he knew. The story was about two cane cutters who, like eagles, flew out of the sun of Queensland to spend three months every year in a terrace house in Melbourne (Carlton, to be exact) with two barmaids. They had done it for sixteen years and this was the seventeenth. His play was so extraordinary for us all because he was a native Australian and it reflected an Australian sensibility quite apart from England. For decades Australia remained hell-bent on trying to imitate England, yet the sense of inferiority remained. Lawler was part of the change that was in the air.

Eventually, I came to play Bubba, the young girl next door in this drama, Ray Lawler's *The Summer of the Seventeenth Doll.* I felt for the first time the joy of using my own Aussie voice and speaking of places that I really knew, and at the same time knowing that the audience had the same experience. No conjuring up or imagining a world not ours. First Melbourne cheered, then Sydney, then all of Australia, and finally London. But nothing will ever be the same as that first time when a veil was lifted and communication was direct. All plays, if they are rooted in their own corner of the world, will speak to all corners of the world.

I learned a university of knowledge those first two seasons with the Union Theatre Rep. I learned that I must know as much as possible about the time my character lived. What she wore and why, what she sat in, and how she sat. What she ate and how she ate it. What was the state of the society she lived in? What was expected of her as a woman, and what was shocking? Did she dance, and if so, how? To research properly you must do a small university course. Fortnightly rep doesn't leave you a lot of time for libraries and galleries, but encyclopedias aren't too bad.

When I played the title role in *Major Barbara* in our second season, I realized I didn't need encyclopedias. Shaw had done it all. He usually does, but as the play is a conflict between the power of money made through munitions manufacturing and the moral force of the Salvation Army to save the poor, I thought a visit to the Salvation Army wouldn't be a bad thing. Also, the conversion in the play of Bill Walker, from cockney bully to reasonable citizen, stumped me. John Sumner had explained that it must be a seduction, but I could not match that quality with the words. So, as Mum went to any church that had rousing hymns, because she loved singing and embarrassed me by singing so boldly, I thought why not give Mum a really good time?

"Mum, would you come with me on Sunday and gather with the Salvation Army band on the corner of Bourke and Swanston Streets and sing our way up Bourke Street to the Citadel?"

"That would be lovely, Zoe, thank you."

Everything was exactly as Shaw wrote it. The big

drum, the tambourines, the Salvation Army uniforms of navy blue with dark red piping, men in smart peak caps, and the gorgeous bonnets of the women with the big ribbon under their chin and tied at the side of their face in a becoming bunch. Once we were seated inside the Citadel, people began to walk to the front and tell us the story of their salvation, between hymns.

One very good-looking young woman, an officer of God's Army—a major—moved easily and quietly through the congregation. Every now and then, she bent down to speak into the ear of a sinner.

I desperately wanted to look full of sin so she would bend down and talk into my ear. And at last she did. She had a lovely voice and smelled good. I told her that I was a visitor from Ballarat, which is north of Melbourne, and that the lady who so enjoyed singing was my aunt. I couldn't say that I was Zoe Caldwell about to play Major Barbara come to research her conversions. Also, the Salvation Army did not endorse Shaw's play. She spoke to me for several minutes and made me feel that I had come to the Citadel to find something to give me the strength to deal with a problem. If I gave myself completely and held nothing back, I would find that strength. I wished to tell her my problem. I wished to rise and be saved, for she was wondrously seductive, but I had come to find Barbara, not

Bill, and she had given me Barbara without mentioning salvation or the Lord or God, but just offering help.

Turning to Mum, I said, "We had better go, Auntie, or we will be late for Uncle Ted."

"Who?" said Mum, who might have stayed and been saved and enjoyed the hot meal. Reluctantly she left with me and we silently caught our tram home.

Sometimes things have to be experienced in spite of punctuation and I am forever grateful to that young woman (maybe it was her bonnet) who showed me how to "convert." I don't have to play Major Barbara again because I got her right the first time. If I have played a part and feel I have fully realized it, I don't need to do it again. However, if I don't feel that I have, it haunts me and I must sing it until I do get it right.

The second thing I learned in fortnightly rep was not to have an affair with an actor of the company, since it created difficulties if I then had to play a love scene onstage with him. Too many personal and private things dancing around that have nothing to do with the script; so much easier to have a clean slate. Then both of you discover the attraction of one character to another in front of the audience, which envelopes them in the intimacy. That's why they have come to the theatre, after all—not to be left out but to be included.

Sex is such a strange thing in the theatre. You can look like a warthog, but if you have talent, you're desirable. Like a prince, however, if no talent, sex flies out the window. There is a great deal of snobbery in the theatre, but it has nothing to do with race, creed, or gender—just talent. I don't know if the same applies to movies, for I know nothing about movies. I just buy my ticket and have a good time. There is one strange difference. I never fall asleep in a movie but only rarely do I remember films. I often fall asleep in the theatre, but when I see a remarkable piece of theatre, I never forget it and it becomes part of my bloodstream.

The third thing I learned was that I needed a larger pool to swim in.

~ 10 ~

The Australian Elizabethan Theatre Trust

THERE was in Australia, in 1954, a remarkable man, Dr. H. C. Coombs, who was the governor of the Commonwealth Bank and an economist in the John Maynard Keynes tradition. He was short, witty, and because of his great mental and physical energy, tremendously attractive. His nickname was Nugget. Nugget Coombs believed, like Keynes, that a country's monetary growth must go hand in hand with its artistic growth. Otherwise you end up with a rich, uncivilized society. To this day, in the United States, I am constantly searching for our Washington "nuggets."

The young Queen Elizabeth II, who was tiny and

prettier than I had imagined, had just visited Australia with her handsome husband, and Dr. Coombs thought that a really great way to commemorate the visit would be to create the Australian Elizabethan Theatre Trust, a national company of theatre, opera, and ballet. It proved to be a huge undertaking and he needed help, which he received from an eclectic but extraordinary group of luminaries, most of them from England. Hugh Hunt, whose brother had climbed Mount Everest with Edmund Hillary, came out to the "colonies" from the Old Vic, as did Robert Quentin. Stephan Haag was from Melbourne, John Sumner, now of Melbourne, Robin Lovejoy from Sydney, and the great Elsie Beyer of Shropshire.

Elsie Beyer, the tiny empress of the West End theatre, had short neat blond hair, very dark glasses, and a soft burr on the end of "dear," a word she favored a lot. She had been a nurse in World War I and one of the wounded she nursed back to life became so dependent upon her that he suggested she work for him after the war. She did, as secretary, assistant, and eventually general manager of his huge West End empire, which he founded in 1936. H. M. Tennent was the king of English theatre and Elsie, because of the power he gave her, was his consort. As with quite a few royal couples, there was nothing physical between them. He was homosexual and doted upon the beautiful young Hugh Beaumont, who at the time didn't seem interested in the theatre. So all three were happy. Elsie was courted, wined and dined, and given many rich gifts—not by lovers, but by actors, directors, and play-wrights. She was mighty shrewd with the writing of con-tracts and mighty swift with the cutting of salaries. All three attended auditions, so I am told.

When Harry Tennent died he left his empire to his companion, Binkie Beaumont, but the management in the hands of Elsie. One day, Binkie, who was to become a truly great entrepreneur, suggested that they should do a particular play, and Elsie said, "No, dear. If you do that play, dear, I would have to leave."

"Then leave," said Binkie.

Her feet barely touched the street before she realized her world had changed. No phone calls, no dinners, no presents. People had feared her and now there was no need. She was a tiny woman with short neat blond hair, very dark glasses, a soft burr on the end of "dear," and no one wanted her.

It was an era when many major English actors came to Australia, and I saw them all. The first to visit were Laurence Olivier and Vivien Leigh, who with the Old Vic Company had conquered Australia in 1948 with their tri-umphant tour, the first after the Second World War.

Richard III, *The School for Scandal*, and *The Skin of Our Teeth* were the plays, and Mum, Dad, and I saw all three. Elsie had been invited by the Oliviers to be the general manager. Elsie liked Australia. Australia liked Elsie. So she stayed and everyone benefited.

I don't know who decided to open the Trust with *Medea* starring Judith Anderson, I only know that I was asked to play the second woman of Corinth. I left home and went to Sydney.

Sydney is, of course, a very exciting city now. It was exciting then too, a little decadent, and it frightened me; but I had a reason for being there and a job to do.

We were an Australian company with the exception of Jason (Clement McCallin). We felt like God's chosen and rehearsed for three weeks without Judith Anderson, using the stage manager's script from the original New York production. Although Hugh Hunt did not like having to follow the directions of John Gielgud, who had done the New York production, Judith insisted on this route. He also did not like Robinson Jeffers's translation of *Medea*. Not many Englishmen do. It is, however, clean, strong, and spare. Robinson Jeffers was the son of a Greek scholar, and as a boy, he had read and spoken ancient Greek. Most English versions are more decorated with Victorian words and rhythms. Moreover, Hugh Hunt was not fond of Judith Anderson, who had been born in Adelaide. When she was in her late teens, her mother took her to America, where she rose to fame working in productions by David Belasco on Broadway, until her Medea shot her into big-time stardom. She played it on tour all across America and in Paris, at the Théâtre Sarah Bernhardt, and now she was bringing it home.

Finally, she arrived like a diva come to sing her role with this company. We practically curtsied. Then, without taking off her high-heeled ankle strap snakeskin shoes (she had lovely legs), or changing out of her honey-colored cashmere sweater and skirt (no bra—in the 1950s!—she had good breasts), she began to rehearse. Immediately we knew that we were not God's chosen. "Move down there. Look at me. Keep your head down. Further back," she instructed as she moved about but all the while speaking no "Medea"—or, if she did, so softly that we never heard it. I think this is called "marking."

After about ten days we packed and moved to Canberra to open in the Albert Hall in front of the Governor General, Sir William Slim; Sir Robert Menzies, the prime minister; the leader of the opposition, Dr. H. V. Evatt; and all the diplomats and politicians you could wish for. If that is what you wish for.

Canberra is the capital of Australia, inland between

Sydney and Melbourne. I'm sure it is a vastly different city now, but in 1955 it bore little resemblance to Sydney; any city whose only employer is the government and only purpose is to govern is bound to be dull.

Anderson's Medea was renowned for its wild, dangerous quality. "Like a tigress," people said. And on that opening night the audience and the company saw "her" Medea. There for the first time was the Castillo gray wool jersey costume, the red wig, the shell and leather bracelets, the sandals, and the voice. Everyone heard her.

I had watched her like a hawk, waiting for her fireworks, and then suddenly she exploded. It was frightening to be onstage with her. But while I had waited, I realized that offstage Judith Anderson was a lonely woman. She had had many lovers, two husbands, no children, a lot of dachshunds, but theatre was her life. And I thought, even as I watched her take her magnetic curtain calls, I can't let that happen to me. It is too heavy a responsibility to make your talent your life, too big a load for talent to bear. Talent then has to fill all your needs, all your desires, and if it doesn't, you are truly alone.

Also, if you are to head a company of actors you must parent it too. Judith didn't know much about parenting, but I genuinely liked her. I didn't learn to love her. That had to wait for nearly thirty years. She was deeply

Australian in love with England—"home," as she called it, but that had to do with her age and the age in which she was raised. She wanted to be a Dame so badly. She was tiny, tough, and spoke with that slightly piss-elegant voice at times, in deference to the Queen, but mostly she used her own marvelous voice with quite a few down-under vowels. I admired her for those vowels. My accent belongs nowhere. I pick up sounds that please me and discard some that don't but if you say "boo," suddenly I have a real Aussie vowel.

Like many tough-minded people, Judith Anderson, from Adelaide, was quite vulnerable too, but you had to watch her, like a hawk, to know.

We were, as a company, treated right royally by the people of Australia. They were thrilled to have their own national theatre headed by an international star who was from Australia. Dinner parties, great picnics in the bush, and packed houses. It was not such a great production but not many mentioned it. They so wanted us to succeed. I felt sad when the *Medea* tour ended and Judith went back to America, to her avocado farm in Santa Barbara, her dogs, and her friends, because I thought that I would never see her again.

I returned to the Union Theatre Rep in Melbourne for one play and then back to Sydney for the rehearsals of the Australian Elizabethan Trust's next tour, which consisted of Sheridan's *The Rivals* and another go at *Twelfth Night*. I was a junior member of the company playing the naughty maid Lucy Locket in the former and Olivia's maid Maria in the latter. Clement McCallin stayed but most of the actors were leading Sydney actors. They were unquestionably skilled and attractive and bold. The company as a result was more colorful and vigorous. I often wondered how they would have dealt with Judith. A Brisbane actress, Jacklyn Kelleher, who had roomed with me on the *Medea* tour and played the third woman of Corinth, married Ray Lawler and I was the maid of honor. I had evolved from throwing petals as a flower girl at the age of two, to carrying the bride's train as train bearer at the age of six, to tending the bride as bridesmaid at the age of eighteen. I had now reached senior status as maid of honor. I supposed someday I would graduate to bride. But not yet.

~ 11 ~

The Wisdom of Elsie

ELSIE BEYER was now the general manager of the theatre part of the Australian Elizabethan Trust, happily involved in taking care of a big boisterous family—our company. Not everyone liked Elsie but they felt her importance and her knowledge. I sensed her keeping an eye on me. Not because she was afraid I might shoplift, although I might, but because I might make dumb professional decisions. Although I liked and trusted her, I was not prepared for her to stop me from going to England.

England was where all young Australian actors wanted

to go because that was where all the important theatre that we saw came from. America didn't send companies to the Antipodes. We did American plays but never saw its leading actors. So England was where we wanted to be and the route was: get to London, wait on tables, and audition.

Lawler's *The Summer of the Seventeenth Doll* had opened in Sydney, setting the city on its ears because that little house in Carlton, Victoria, could have been in Woolloomooloo, New South Wales. The people were the same funny, rough, romantic lot who would rather have a kewpie doll on a stick than a gold band on the fourth finger of their left hand. These women had three months of wild romance and then the men would fly away. That was their life and they didn't want it shattered. In a very male-dominated country, those two barmaids were in charge of their lives. But it couldn't last.

We now had Shakespeare, Sheridan, and Lawler on our tour number two. Jackie Lawler was playing Bubba in *The Doll* and rooming with Ray (appropriately, as they were married) when she became pregnant with twins, and I was given Bubba to play. I understood Bubba Ryan because she was to the barmaids, Olive and Pearl, and their men, Barney and Roo, what I had been to the English children, to Zillah and Joan and Phyllis and Nettie and Spider and

Macka. My name was Zoe and those neighbors called me Judy. Her name was Kathie and her neighbors called their little pet from next door, Bubba, meaning baby. When the play begins she is eighteen and ready to become Kathie. I was Bubba when the word came that Olivier wanted to bring the play to London under his management.

We were all elated and cheering: "*London*! *The West End*! *Laurence Olivier*!"

Elsie asked me to have lunch with her at a little Chinese restaurant near the theatre, where she told me that I would not be going to London. There was a long pause.

"Why?"

"Because, dear, if you go as Bubba, dear, you will be thought of as an Australian actress, dear."

"That's great."

"No, dear, it's not. You will be playing in an indigenously Australian play using a strong Australian accent. You have not experienced typecasting, which makes you very lucky and a bit cocky. You think you can play any part given you, and I think you can too, but we may be the only two who do. You will not get to play the parts I want you to play. The parts you want to play. You *will* go to England—I will see to that, dear, but simply as an actress."

"When?"

"You will do one more Trust tour, dear, which will give me time to work everything out."

End of lunch, dear.

It's funny how the young feel that things must be done now, or time will run out. The older you get and the less time you have, the more prepared you are to wait and have patience.

I knew that Elsie really cared and that she was right, but I thought that was the end of England for me. However, I trusted Elsie, so I finished the tour, threw streamers at the *Doll* company as it sailed away, returned to the Union Theatre Rep for one more play and then back to Sydney for the third Trust tour—Miss Hoyden in Vanbrugh's *The Relapse* and Ophelia in Paul Roger's *Hamlet*, directed by Hugh Hunt. Paul is a darling man, a marvelous actor, but not a Hamlet. He knew he was not. He is very bright. But as he said, it was his only chance to play Hamlet and you don't let that go. He was wicked and stunning in *The Relapse*. He and his wife, Roz Boxall, led the company well and I learned that I had better have another go at Ophelia, for I sure didn't bring her to life the first time. I was young and pretty and my mad scene was very good. However, all the scenes leading to the mad scene—the life that is lived before madness that makes madness inevitable—were empty. So many of Shakespeare's young girls are without the presence of a mother: Miranda in *The Tempest*, Viola in *Twelfth Night*, Desdemona in *Othello*, but the one that seems the most lost is Ophelia, and she would haunt me until I got her right.

Nine months later I was back at the Union Theatre Rep playing in Ugo Betti's *The Queen and the Rebels* when Elsie asked me again to lunch, this time in the very elegant dining room of the Melbourne hotel where she lived. She was back from England and she was elated. *The Summer of the Seventeenth Doll* had been a triumph at London's St. James Theatre. She had also met with Glen Byam Shaw and had arranged a contract for me with the Shakespeare Memorial Theatre in Stratford-upon-Avon of which he was the director. It was to walk on, understudy, or play in their next season, which would open April 8, 1958. I would be paid twelve pounds a week and I must be there at the beginning of February.

"I have arranged with Dr. Coombs, dear, for the Australian government to pay your fare. You will travel in a six-berth cabin in the bottom of the *Oronsay*, dear."

"As ballast?"

And we laughed because we both realized what a miracle she had wrought.

Part Two

1958–1965

~ 12 ~

Journey from Down Under

WHEN I told Mum and Dad the news that I would be going to England, they could hardly believe it. Mum said I would need new clothes and she had better start right away making them. Dad said I would need some new suitcases and he had better go down to Port Melbourne, to the shipping line of the Pacific and Orient and study the plans of the *Oronsay*. Not that he could have changed anything but Dad loved ships and anything to do with them. Also, he was the only person I've ever known who never became seasick. Perhaps he should have gone in my place. There was a flurry of activity, from packing to putting things in trunks to go under the house. We didn't have attics and went under the house to store things. At last my two suit-cases were packed in the boot (trunk) of the Peugeot, and after I had run up and down Yongala Street saying good-bye to our neighbors, we drove to the Melbourne docks. The *Oronsay* was filled with passengers all standing on one side of the ship. Dad said he would help me stow my luggage while Mum said she would remain with Bert. I knew that Dad just wanted to go on board and look at my cabin, and after he had looked around, we went back to Mum, and he said, "I think she'll be all right, Mum. She'll have a lot of company." We all laughed and held one another. Then I walked up the gangplank to the lowest deck and threw streamers to my mother, my father, and my brother, all of us weeping and waving until the ship slowly pulled away from the pier and the streamers broke.

We had a journey of six weeks ahead of us, incredible when compared to today, so I thought I had best go down to the cabin and meet my cabin mates. One Australian girl I knew. We had planned to travel together. Her name was Peg Cherry and her husband, Wal, had asked me to keep an eye on her. I chose to keep my boss eye on her, so she had a great time. The other passengers sleeping in our cabin were four disgruntled Pommies, an Aussie word for English immigrants, who were going back home after a couple of years hard labor. The whole of steerage, other than Peg and me, consisted of people from Europe running away from Australia and complaining that Australia was not England, not Italy, not Greece.

Our cabin was small, very small, and there was nowhere that the complaints of our four Englishwomen could escape, so they ricocheted from wall to wall. Then I got seasick and decided to go on deck, if need be for the whole journey. Peg got some pills from the ship's doctor, which really worked, and Peg and I made our plan. We would go to the cabin straight after dinner, while our ladies were drinking it up and dancing, and then get up as soon as they came down and go up on deck to sleep. We tried not to breathe as we ran past the hold full of sheepskins on their way to Europe. There was a pool on deck, but so many people jumped in and out all day that the water didn't look particularly inviting. At 3:00 A.M., the crew would empty it, clean it, and fill it with fresh seawater. Then just the two of us swam, showered, dressed, and sat in the deck chairs to watch the sun rise. At six-thirty, we would then have breakfast and be back on deck with our books by nine.

I found reading difficult because there was so much humanity to observe. Actors need to observe, for that is what they draw upon. To observe and engage other humans—old, young, rich, poor, in any country of the world—is essential. So, the *Oronsay* turned out to be my gold mine. Not only was the ship full of people from all rungs of society, of all ages, but of all nationalities too. Here, I didn't have to become Sue Vale. Peg and I were a pretty anonymous pair and most people enjoyed engaging us in conversation. We got to know most of steerage and the steerage crew rather well. Six weeks is a long time.

When we docked in Singapore, I had a swim in the fluorescent waters off Changi Prison with a beautiful young Eurasian man who had taken Peg and me around the city, and the ship nearly left without us. Four of the crew took us to a wild nightclub in Barcelona, where the most beautiful creatures in gorgeous gowns danced and stripped—all men. This was a first for me. The ship had many Greeks returning home and an equal number of Greek Cypriots, which kept the air alive with hostility, and I felt quite fearless in my choosing an Athenian Greek for romance.

I even learned to like our cabin mates. When you see people hurling the remains of bad lobster stew around the cabin and you clean everything up, including them, you do tend to become bonded.

We stopped at ten ports before we came to rest at Southampton, but two memories remain particularly vivid. After leaving Aden, the ship went up the Red Sea and through the Suez Canal. First I could not believe how narrow the channel was and how close the people on either bank were. The English had launched an attack on Egypt to regain full dominion over the canal only two years before and we were a British ship. The *Oronsay*'s engines were cut off and we were pulled through the narrow strip of water. Absolute silence. Nobody spoke, although everyone was on deck, and nobody moved. There was just a high-pitched electrical whine cutting the silence our whole way past the hostile Egyptians, who stood motionless, also not speaking, on either side.

The second memory is the sweet pipe of the umbrella man very early in the morning in Lisbon. He wasn't selling; he was merely mending umbrellas and the music from his pipe let us know that he and his cart were there.

All too soon, we arrived in Southampton.

～ 13 ～

England

"LONDON pride had been handed down to me." The street where our bed-and-breakfast had stood for a long time made me understand Christopher Robin. Everything in London—the parks, the shops, the buses, the postboxes, the policemen, and, of course, the guard changing at Buckingham Palace—was absolutely part of my life and yet totally foreign. I recognized everything and knew nothing. I don't know how typical this is for Australians coming to London for the first time, but this is exactly what I felt.

After two days, I bid farewell to Peg, who was joining her husband, who had flown over, and boarded my train to Stratford. I was bursting with nervous excitement but no one else in my compartment spoke or got caught looking. Eventually one very conservative-looking man folded his *Times*, put it in his briefcase, and asked me where I was from. He told me he was an accountant from Birmingham, and he, his wife, and family, the Nettles, became my first real friends in England.

I had been advised by Stratford that I would have a room in the house of a Miss Beecham, formerly of Leamington Spa, now of Shottery Road, Stratford. I arrived, with my two suitcases, at a two-up, two-down (two rooms upstairs, two rooms down) house with a little garden front and back and a hedge and a gate. Beechie, as I quickly learned to call her, opened the front door and said, "Oh, I'm going to have to fatten you up." She wasn't smiling. She was worried. I was five foot three and 105 pounds. But from the moment she opened the door, I was hers, her responsibility, and she would take care of me. This had nothing to do with me. She cared the same for whomever lived in her house. She had only one actor at a time but sometimes they stayed for years. She was a truly maidenly lady of seventy, slim with white hair, and I was hers for one year. I would grow to love her deeply.

Shakespeare Memorial Theatre was not "royal" in 1958, but it was the home of the royals of the theatre. Then, as now, it sits upon the Avon River like a large bulky building that was put there by mistake, but buildings have a way of settling in and looking as though they have always been there. Of course, what really matters is what goes on inside. Michael Redgrave headed that year's company, which was of a high order. Glen Byam Shaw, Tony Richardson, Peter Hall, and Douglas Seale directed; Tanya Moiseiwitsch, the Motley trio, Lila De Nobili, and Loudon Sainthill designed; and Leslie Bridgewater, Roberto Gerhard, Antony Hopkins, and Christopher Whelan made the music. The actors came in three groups: stars earned sixty pounds a week and big billing; splendid actors eighteen to twenty pounds a week and middle billing; and we twelve pounds a week and tiny print.

All this was as it should be and the only mystery was why should I be there at all. To learn, of course, to watch and learn and walk on and off, to the best of my ability. The fact that I had had such big responsibilities for the last four years was a big advantage. I knew how much I knew. I knew how much I had to learn and I was also quite critical of what I was seeing.

The first play was *Hamlet* and Glen Byam Shaw, a most elegant man, did a rather old-fashioned heavy production with Michael Redgrave as Hamlet and Googie Withers as Gertrude. Michael was very tall and a little old for Hamlet, but an extraordinary thing happened toward the end of the season. The directors for the next season were invited to see the present plays played by understudies with full lighting, props, and, if you got the principal's permission, costumes.

Ian Holm, a short, exciting actor, understudied Michael and, because of the difference in height, had to have costumes made to fit him. Every other actor was roughly the size of his or her principal. Suddenly, into the middle of a large, tall court came a perfect, young, small prince and the play became riveting. That one element changed everyone's emotional response. We cared for that young prince, understood his vulnerability and his obsession with something being rotten in the State of Denmark. We felt he was in danger and we wanted to help.

The second production was a young, lovely *Twelfth Night* with Geraldine McEwan's deliciously witty Olivia and Dorothy Tutin and Ian Holm as Viola and Sebastian, but without Barry Humphries's Orsino. The designer was the magical Lila De Nobili and the director, Peter Hall. I loved watching that production unfold.

Lila De Nobili, I learned, was an Italian artist, a painter as well as a designer, and she actively engaged in how a certain look was achieved right up to and sometimes even during opening night. Her colors were rustic golds, browns, reds, and the smock she wore to paint in became indistinguishable from the set because her brushes were always at work and dripping. I never spoke to her but I watched her constantly.

Geraldine McEwan had—and still does have—a strange voice that would be irritating if it weren't so winning and she so gifted.

Dorothy Tutin has recently become a Dame and Ian Holm a Knight. Geraldine is one of the few undecorated British actors around of our generation. Thus, she has become a member of a tiny elite club.

The next play was *Pericles*, one of the rarely done Shakespeare plays. Pericles was the head of the city-state of Athens in fifth-century B.C. Greece. He roamed the world, made a lot of mistakes, and to atone for them, built the Acropolis as, if you will, a WPA venture. It is a wild story and Tony Richardson was clearly the man to direct it.

He was six foot three, thin, with ears that you were aware of, and a voice you could never forget. It was a combination of North Country, Oxford, and slow. Richardson was brilliant, perhaps a little mad, compassionate and full of humor. When we first met he greeted me with, "I want you to play the incestuous Daughter of Antiochus. It's going to be absolutely marvelous. You will be carried naked on a bier, painted green. You painted green, not the bier." Of course I couldn't be naked—the theatre's Board of Governors and the Lord Chancellor, who licensed all British theatrical productions, would never have allowed it then. But I was painted green.

Tony's next challenge for us was the three Mycenian whores, played by Pam Taylor, Eileen Atkins, and me. Mycenian whores, Tony told us, were riddled with syphilis and exposed their breasts. Fair enough. Our faces were made up to be pretty whorish but no amount of syphilitic makeup could turn our breasts Mycenian. Six perfectly upturned breasts made a joke of the wonderful clothes, scenery, and lighting. Eventually, we wore rubber breasts that turned people's stomachs, but made us feel totally fine. Each of us walk-ons played about ten different parts in *Pericles*, so there was much running up and down the stairs and bumping into one another backstage, changing costumes, makeup, and breasts. It was very good training for practically anything. You didn't need to work out. Tony Richardson kept your blood racing.

To help the audience know where they are in *Pericles*, there is a character named Gower who, like a chorus, speaks and sometimes sings the story. Tony Richardson had wanted Paul Robeson for the part. Unfortunately, he was ill and a West Indian singer came instead and constantly lectured us on racial injustices and our racist attitudes. We felt guilty and cowered and were much relieved that Paul hadn't come. Paul Robeson was a world-renowned figure who had spoken out against racial injustice eloquently and often, and had had his passport taken from him because of it. We doubted we would have survived if it had been Paul. When he did come the next season to play Othello, we realized how wrong we were.

In fair Verona, where we lay our scene, a pair of star-crossed lovers take their lives. They are the youngest of all Shakespeare's lovers, the most poetic and along with Hamlet, the characters that young people all over the world can most identify with. It is essential that they be young and passionate. Glen Byam Shaw directed a beautiful production, classically beautiful, but lacking the dangerous excitement of youth. The mistakes that lead to death would not have been made by this group of citizens. Dorothy Tutin was a young, beautiful Juliet and Richard Johnson was Romeo. They made the fatal mistake of really falling in love, so they had a grand time and the audience was left out in the cold.

Michael Redgrave was a complex, gentle man, and a friend, with an American assistant named Fred Sadoff with whom I got along famously. Googie Withers was irresistible. Googie had played Gertrude in *Hamlet* and now was Beatrice to Michael's Benedick in Douglas Seale's *Much Ado About Nothing*. I was asked to play

Margaret, who is a maid of honor, and I knew how to play that.

Tanya Moiseiwitsch gave us clothes, as she always does, never costumes, and slipped our feet into flat slippers so the Victorian crinolines floated over the stage—except for Googie, who insisted on keeping her high heels. The men looking stunning in their uniforms, all fell for the right ladies in the end, but of course there was much ado about everything.

I realized quite soon that none of the actors was much interested in watching the other actors. Most seemed to feel that they could have done it better if they had been given the chance, so why bother observing rehearsals. I felt otherwise. My old hawk eye along with my boss eye watched everything, even the things that were not illuminating or exciting to find out why they were not. There was a lot of knitting and reading of the newspaper in the rehearsal room, something Tyrone Guthrie would put a stop to when he arrived the next year for the great celebratory hundredth-year season. If you were in the rehearsal room, you watched the rehearsal and Guthrie made sure that you had a good time doing it. He believed all energies in a room must be involved in the play. If you didn't like that, go outside.

I shared a dressing room way upstairs with Pam

Taylor, who was much more interested in her newly married housewifely self than throwing on a few costumes and walking on (she was not asked back); Mavis Edwards, a tiny sprite of a woman with white hair and bright eyes, who had been at Stratford for two seasons; and Eileen Atkins, whose beginnings were similar to mine (reasonably poor; toe, tap, and ballet; elocution and concerts and medals). One thing set her apart from us all. She was a true cockney, born within the sound of the Bow Bells, and because her mother was forty-five when she gave birth to Eileen, no German bombs were going to part them. So, unlike other children Eileen stayed in the center of London all through the war. Neurotic she was, and understandably so, but she was funny, really funny, bright, and talented. She became my friend and has remained my friend to this day. I loved her mum. We share a birthday—a few years apart—but each year when I was in England I visited with flowers, on our birth date. And the visits were long because her mum was so witty. She remained in that little house in Courtman Road, Tottenham, until she died at the age of ninety-four.

One day toward the end of the season Eileen invited me to spend a day with her at the spa at Leamington Spa, twenty minutes away by train. She said she made a point of going at the end of a season to clean out her pores. And that's how it happened. Eileen and I were sitting on a wooden bench in the steam room surrounded by fat ladies who were reading wet newspapers. We were all naked. Nobody spoke. Suddenly we realized that the ladies were moving as far along the benches as possible to be as far from us as possible. Why? They were fat, we were thin— no need to ostracize. But at the same moment Eileen and I looked down at our bodies. There were Eileen's pores ridding themselves of a colorless accumulated sweat while mine were oozing dark green. Tony Richardson and the Daughter of Antiochus were having a field day. That's the sort of humiliation you get when you are given such a showy part to play when you are really a walk-on.

Suddenly everyone was talking about the Green Room Rag. I had no idea what they meant. I knew the green room was where actors wait to rehearse, or go onstage, or read, or just loll about. There is usually food and drink and a lot of gossip. It is sometimes painted green. But Green Room Rag? Then Eileen told me that once a year all the people backstage, in the costume departments, props, jack hats and his merry men, who made all the hats (and in Shakespeare, there are a lot of hats), those who took care of the front of house and the restaurants and the grounds, were given a party and entertained by us, the company.

Eileen and I decided that we would put together a tap routine to "Mairzy Doats," which you would know now only if you are on your way to seventy. It was a silly song but easy to tap to. We practiced hard in our borrowed tap shoes and bought pretty little white blouses at Woolworths and a lot of red crepe paper, out of which we made tiny pleated skirts, ruffles around the back of our white panties, big bows on our tap shoes, and a big bow in our hair. Our hair we set in curls à la Shirley Temple. We were a smash and had to come back twice.

I learned a great deal that first season. Some of it at the theatre, but mostly from living with Beechie in Shottery. I realized how important the change of seasons was to your spirit, which made me understand all the rituals I had grown up with. The connection of the earth with life and religion made sense. Celebrations like Easter, harvest festival, and Guy Fawkes Day corresponded to what was happening to the earth. Easter, spring, new growth; harvest festival, harvest the land and share it; Guy Fawkes Day, dead leaves to be burnt. In Australia, Easter is in autumn; our harvest festival, in spring at the time of the beginning of growth; and Christmas comes in hell-hot summer. No wonder I was confused. We are so far from the source but dancing the

Edgar Caldwell, c. 1919

Zoe Hivon c. 1919

Bert, Mum, Dad and Zoe. The family, 1934

Winifred Moverly Browne and her husband, John Alexander Browne, 1940

Beechie, 1958

Elsie Beyer, 1956

Ailsa Grahame, Zoe Caldwell and Jacklyn Kelleher as the three Women of Corinth and Judith Anderson as Medea in Medea. *The Australian Elizabethan Theater Trust, 1954*

Albert Finney as Cassio and Zoe as Bianca, in Othello. *Shakespeare Memorial Theater, Stratford-upon-Avon, 1959*

Company of Three Sisters. *Guthrie Theater, Minneapolis, 1963*

Hume Cronyn as Harpagon and Zoe as Frosine in The Miser.
Guthrie Theater Minneapolis, 1963

Zoe as Gruscha, The Caucasian Chalk Circle. *Guthrie Theater, Minneapolis, 1965*

Alan Bates as Richard III and Zoe as Lady Anne, in Richard III. *Festival Theater, Stratford, Ontario, 1967*

Zoe as Cleopatra in Antony and Cleopatra. *Festival Theater, Stratford, Ontario, 1967*

same jigs. I remember, as a little girl, gluing white cotton balls on our windows as pretend snow and eating turkey and plum pudding and brandy sauce in 105 degrees. "Remember, remember the fifth of November," as we danced around a huge pile of burning tires, with a foul acrid smell and us in our bathing suits, licking ice cream cones. That fall of 1958, I cried when I saw the children from the council houses on Shottery Road collect leaves, make a great bonfire of nature's sweet-smelling leftovers, and burn the straw Guy Fawkes. This Guy had sat on a little cart for the preceding week, outside the railway station. "Pennies for the Guy" was the cry in the air. The night was dark, very cold, and they looked so cherubic in their red scarves, caps, and mitts, but at the same time wildly pagan.

Rituals without human need make no sense. Maybe that is what I was seeking when I became so religious at the age of eleven. "I want rituals. Help me make them make sense." And here in Stratford-upon-Avon they did.

All this time, darling Beechie was fattening me up with Yorkshire pudding, bread and butter, cake, sandwiches, jam and clotted cream for tea, and—as a consequence—slowing me down. I was wont to ride my bike at great speed to the theatre, but as my weight increased I could barely make it there at all. Everyone noticed, especially the wardrobe, for I was now 140 pounds, 35 pounds heavier than when Beechie had first opened her door to me.

I didn't have the heart to scold Beechie. She was so pleased that everyone could see how well she was looking after me. She, mysteriously, was getting thinner, which worried me, so I went to Farmer Goodall for advice. He lived up the road and was a true *Milly-Molly-Mandy* character who grew vegetables for all his neighbors and flowers for the church festivals. (Milly, Molly, Mandy was the little girl at the center of an extended family in a thatched roofed cottage, in a tiny village in Warwickshire. There were three books, a map of the village, and I gobbled them up when I was six. Now at twenty-four I was having elderberry wine with two of the characters, Farmer and Mrs. Goodall.) I loved to hear them speak because I knew that their speech was the speech of Shakespeare. Short *a*'s, as in bath and path; pronounced *r*'s, as in sister, brother; full *o*'s, as in gold, cold. Those Hanoverian kings, with their King's English, sure played havoc with the sounds of Shakespeare. However, today in areas of the Blue Ridge Mountains in the United States of America you can still hear the sounds of the Goodalls. They had lived in Warwickshire all their lives and they didn't worry about my getting fat but they did worry about Beechie's thinness. So I went to Beechie's old doctor, who put me on a strict diet, which Beechie felt was a betrayal, and I told him I thought Beechie was ill. He insisted that I bring her to see him. Since her relatives were all in Northumberland, I was in effect her closest relative.

Of course, it was cancer. After opening her up, they declared there was nothing they could do, but she could live another six months, in pain. So now the tables were turned. I had to take care of my darling Beechie.

By then, we were all busy in rehearsals to polish up *Hamlet, Romeo and Juliet,* and *Twelfth Night.* The Soviet Union had invited us to be "Angeliski Artists Stratforde Memorial Theatre" and present our three plays in Moscow and Leningrad (St. Petersburg). This was 1958 so we were privileged to be allowed in. The Iron Curtain had been lifted a bit only the year before.

I would get up early in the morning, bathe Beechie, put her in a clean nightie, straighten her bed, brush her hair, get her some hot porridge and some tea, and pedal off to the theatre for rehearsal. Then I returned to give Beechie some soup and back to rehearsal, a small supper with Beechie, the night performance, and then home. "Are you home for the night?" Beechie would ask like a little girl. "Yes, darling, I'm here for the night." Until one night the pain was so intense that I rang an ambulance and she was in hospital under heavy sedation. We had three weeks to go before Russia. I had access to Beechie's room at the hospital day and night. One night she was conscious and gave me her little old leather purse with ten pounds in it, we kissed on the lips, and then she was gone. This was the first time I had seen death and I was amazed at how gentle it was.

I rang her relatives in Northumberland, packed as many things as I could, and came down with a blinding fever. I collapsed on the bed and might have been there for about forty-eight hours before I was awakened by Judy Wright. Judy, one of our stage managers whom I had never really known, had realized I was missing and came to Beechie's. She stayed for three nights, going back to the theatre when needed, and got me well.

Our departure date was looming. "Have you got a cocktail dress and high-heeled shoes?" Judy asked. "You are going to need them in Russia. They are big party-givers." We went to Birmingham and bought some clothes and then having packed the rest of my stuff, I said good-bye to Shottery Road. I didn't know who I was or where I was and I didn't really care.

It was only natural for Judy to take over. She was a classy girl, born in India, schooled in Switzerland, and able to speak four languages. I spoke one. Instead of being presented at court, she went to London Academy of

Music and Dramatic Arts (LAMDA) to become a stage manager. An actress her mother could have lived with, but a stage manager? Yes, that is what Judy wanted and that is what she became and she was one of the best. Mr. and Mrs. Wright, back from India, lived off Sloane Square in Knightsbridge and were charming, civilized people whom I eventually got to know very well. They welcomed Judy's disoriented friend and spoiled us for the two days before we caught our plane to Moscow. Judy showed me London, which was very beautiful with its Christmas hat on, a city filled with carols being sung by human voices in the streets, not those tired old drummer boys droning mechanically on throughout the stores. I know now—really know—*A Christmas Carol*, which I can almost recite by heart. After a whole season of not knowing each other, Judy and I forged a friendship, which has lasted forty-two years and counting.

As we boarded the plane for Russia, I realized that just as I had begun to understand one foreign country, I was on my way to a truly foreign country, one that I might never understand.

~ 14 ~

Russia

MOSCOW was foreign and cold, so cold that my nose bled. Shops were practically nonexistent, with not much to buy in those that were there, and no Christmas trees, of course. But the Russians had just put a second Sputnik satellite into space so there were many decorated Sputniks for *s novim godom* (the new year). All churches were museums to remind the citizens that there was a time, before the Revolution, when ignorant people prayed to the statue of a weak man on a cross and his mother. There were no carolers singing in the street. The buildings were mainly ugly modern cement boxes "made by Soviet workmen"—except for the Kremlin, with its foreboding wall rising out of Red Square, telling us of the power and strength that has been Russia since Ivan the Terrible. The Byzantine onion domes of St. Basil, the theatres, the opera houses, the Bolshoi, the old wooden houses (starry dom), and the glorious Metropole Hotel, which dwelled in the middle of Moscow in its own time. Heavy velvet and damask at the windows, heavy carpets on the floor, and heavy canopies over heavy beds. Who cared about dust? The lighting was not to read by, but who was reading? There was too much to take in. The chandeliers were large, beautiful, even if they were bugged. We had no secrets, except who was running from one room to another in the middle of the night, and I hardly thought the KGB would care about that.

The Russian actors were "men" and "women" properly dressed and brilliant when they acted. In contrast, we seemed a very ordinary lot, with the exception of Glen Byam Shaw, who was a big hit. His white hair, moustache, graceful clothes, and manners made him stand out as a gentleman, which he was. The Russian women treated him like a star. I think they were used to more bulk in their men. He kissed their hands and they almost swooned when he came out onstage after a performance.

On the flip side we had Coral Browne, who was now playing Gertrude. Coral was a very elegant woman with an Australian accent and the mouth of a truck driver. It was a colorful combination and sometimes people couldn't believe what they'd heard. She spent quite a lot of time in Moscow with Guy Burgess, the English diplomat who, with Donald Maclean, received asylum from their Russian spymasters. Coral did not swap secrets but took Burgess's measurements for all the things that he yearned for, mainly obtainable on Savile Row or Bond Street. Michael Redgrave had gone to Cambridge with Burgess and introduced him to Coral, who brought him to the theatre, where we all met him. He did seem a little sad.

The difference between British and Russian acting was clearly demonstrated by our ball scene in *Romeo and Juliet* and the great ball in the unforgettable film of the ballet *Romeo and Juliet* with Galina Ulanova. We wore jewel-bright silks and satins, while their guests wore heavy, dark velvets and damask. When they danced to Prokofiev, they were important men and women at a ball, of course a Russian ball, even though the play is set in fair Verona.

We were treated royally and were given the best of everything the Russians had. Great bowls of caviar, endless shots of vodka while we drank to the health of our two great nations. This was two years after the Twentieth Soviet Communist Party Congress of 1956, during which Nikita Khrushchev revealed openly the murderous nightmare of Stalin's power. That changed somewhat the feeling of oppression to one of greater freedom, but did not relieve the subsistent level of the lives of most people.

At one reception, three of the actors from the Moscow Arts Theatre did scenes from Shakespeare, and they were extraordinary. They do indeed understand Shakespeare and so do the Soviet audiences. We were told that some thirty or more permanent touring companies toured Russia playing only Shakespeare. That may have been a boast, but the audiences seemed to be ahead of us, sometimes laughing before the joke, and warm and generous to a fault. They clapped, they cheered, they stood. They threw flowers, watches, and eventually jewels, which they stripped from their own bodies. We clapped them, blew kisses, stretched out our arms, until it looked as if we might be there all night. I don't think we were that good but perhaps their apartments were very cold. We never had the same effect on British audiences.

I marveled at the Russians' ability to become the character they played. The only disappointment I felt was that we were never shown any modern plays by new playwrights. I can only think that they wanted to show us their best and that they hadn't yet mastered new writings because at the heart of new writing is always criticism of the status quo. In Russia, then, that was not so easy.

I remember one reception when we had their best

actors perform for us with not one of our leading players returning the compliment. Eileen and I were pushed by the company to do our triumphant tap dance from the Green Room Rag, "Mairzy Doats." We were wearing cocktail dresses (fashionably mid-calf), with high-heeled shoes, and our hair was coifed. We had also drunk to the health of our two great nations quite a lot. The company laughed, but the Russians were properly stunned and Eileen and I were embarrassed. It was the last thing we wanted to do and it was insulting.

St. Petersburg was called Leningrad when we were there, and the city was very much Moscow's beautiful young sister. Moscow was ancient, heavy, and dark. Peter the Great, hoping to bring European culture to his feudal Russia, had had his city designed with eighteenth-century elegance and light to make bearable the long hard winters. Forty years after my visit, I remember the beauty of Leningrad with the frozen Neva making tinkling sounds as the ice cracked, the pale pastel French architecture, and the thought of Hitler's army having tried to decimate it. I remember the courage of the Russian people putting up with so little, so the future would benefit. This was the Party line, but they strongly believed it.

I remember the underground subway in Moscow with its paintings, mosaics, and sculptures going four sta-

tions to the left and four stations to the right. And spot-
less. Drop a gum wrapper or spit and you were fined on
the spot. I remember the sweetness and warmth of the
Russian people and their yearning to communicate and
learn about the outside world. I remember being asked to
leave the Ukraine Hotel because a Reuters correspondent
had taken me to his room for illicit purposes.

And I remember Michael Redgrave sitting cross-
legged on the floor of my room in the Metropole, holding
a tiny wooden candle holder with a tiny wooden candle,
singing "Away in a Manger." I had bought some boxes of
holders and candles and invited the company in to sing
carols on Christmas Eve in case they felt homesick.

Following the monthlong tour of the USSR, the company flew to London, but I went to Copenhagen. Ray and
Jackie Lawler were living there with their twin boys,
beautiful sweet boys, and they had invited me to stay for
the six weeks between Russia and the big new season at
Stratford. I knew that I was going back because Glen
Byam Shaw had told me so before our trip to Russia, over
a glass of sherry up in his small but comfortable office in
Stratford. It was the tradition—I don't know what happens now that the company is Royal—but every member
of the company was invited for a glass of sherry in Glen's
office and told his or her place in the next season, where

you could accept or reject his offer. Miraculously, I was told that I would play Bianca in Paul Robeson's *Othello*, directed by Tony Richardson; Helena in *All's Well That Ends Well*, with Dame Edith Evans, directed by Tyrone Guthrie; and Cordelia to Charles Laughton's Lear, directed by Glen Byam Shaw himself. Moreover, my salary would go to eighteen pounds a week with middle billing. I hope I thanked him, for I just remember stumbling down the stairs, numb with excitement, to be asked, "What did you get?" by the other actors.

At the end of January 1959, I was living on the Rungsted Strandway, which runs along the coast to Elsinore, with two of my oldest friends. We played with the little boys, cooked dinner, and talked. Our lives were very different now. A film had been made of *The Summer of the Seventeenth Doll*, so Ray had money as well as a family. He was writing for the BBC and based in Europe. I was still single, with no money, and based in Stratford.

Jackie and Ray took me to Copenhagen and bought me a Dansk heavy specimen vase, which I still see every day in the bathroom of my house, and three tiny Dansk birds. I saw the Little Mermaid statue but the sight that made the greatest impression was the Kronborg Castle at Elsinore, which truly shocked me. I had played in two productions of *Hamlet*, and seen many more, and never was I aware of the constant presence of the sea except for a moment on a cliff in Olivier's film. The castle itself was rather small and elegant, not Gothic and spooky. The ground floor had large black and white marble tiles and long windows, which let in the light and the changing moods of the sea. Sounds were always present. Ocean sounds, sea bird sounds. Also, being exposed to the ocean on three sides made you realize how vulnerable it was, how necessary those guards on the ramparts were, and how lonely it could be to be so cut off from the rest of the world. Lonely for a little boy called Hamlet and his beautiful young mother called Gertrude. Sure she was the queen but of what? When her husband, the king, was at home with his army, much banqueting and dancing and lovemaking, but like so many CEOs or leaders of countries, he had to be away conquering and making deals with not much time for the kid or indeed his wife. Do you wonder that Gertrude fell into the warm arms of Claudius? Do you wonder that the teenaged Hamlet, estranged from his father and cut off from his mother who, before Claudius, had made him the center of her life, now seemed a rather moody young prince? Of course, there was Ophelia, whom he loved, but they had been in each other's company since they could walk. Best pack the boy off to the university at Wittenberg. He'll be better with young male friends.

I longed to see a production of *Hamlet* with the sea the main feature.

Ray and Jackie were getting irritated with my endless talk about *Hamlet* and I had only two more weeks before I left for Stratford. "Forget *Hamlet*," Ray said. "Try your mind on *Othello* and *All's Well That Ends Well* and *Lear*. It will be a relief for us."

I had been in *Othello*, seen *Lear*, but *All's Well* was new to me. I'll start with it, I thought. But when I opened the paperback copy, all I could see was Helena, Helena, Helena. "Ray," I shouted, "she's got so many *soloquies*!"

"The word is *soliloquies* and you have your work cut out."

And I did.

Upon my return to Stratford, I had quickly to find digs. This was now the world without Beechie. I went in the other direction from Shottery—Tiddington and at the back of a farm called Elms Farm, I found a tiny house on the river, a shack really. Elms Farm, Tiddington— sounds like a place for an elf. Well, I was short and thin again, and because Judy had gone to Canada, I asked Mavis Edwards, the tiny, sweet-faced woman with white hair who had shared the dressing room last season, whether she would consider becoming a fellow elf. "I'd love it," she said. And so we were two. The bike ride to the theatre was twice as long, but I had no intention of putting on weight again. I would be able to ride speedily.

Only one year before, I had arrived in England. I had experienced a second upbringing in that one year. I had assumed I would be a stronger, wiser actress by now. I don't think I was, but I knew I was already a much stronger, wiser woman.

~ 15 ~

The Great Season

THERE was little question that the 1959 season would be different. *Othello* was the first production, and we all nervously awaited the arrival of Paul Robeson from Russia. Paul was, in so many ways, a giant of a man. All his life he had excelled—as an athlete, a scholar, a singer—and, because he seemed to have no fear, he spoke out against injustice wherever he found it. I think envy had a great deal to do with his being driven from his own country. He was a Gulliver among us Lilliputians. He spoke to everyone in the same voice, no matter how grand the person, no matter how small. And never once did he mention race. And he smelled so good as he swept down the halls in his long robes. He was very attractive to women. Could be a description of Othello.

Iago is, of course, the driving force of *Othello* because it is his NCO (non-commissioned officer) rage at feeling passed over and unnoticed by high-born men not his equal that drives him to plot their downfall. This is not an unusual feeling among NCOs, but usually they don't take their revenge that far. I think it is important that Iago's plans unfold before us as we are watching. It is a mistake to make him evil from the start. Also, it makes Othello seem not very bright if it is clear that Iago means him ill.

The American actor Sam Wanamaker was our Iago. He had arrived in England several years before distinctly uneasy about the atmosphere surrounding the House Un-American Activities Committee. He too, had a boss eye, but managed to conceal it by never switching his look from left to right without first lowering his head. I do the same thing. He was clearly successful. His energy was considerable. He worked out, which was unusual for the time, rode a speed bike, and kayaked the river at all times of day. He taught the company, both women and men, to play baseball. The Stratford company was renowned for its cricket. In fact, better to be a good wicket keeper than a Brutus. So you can understand his perseverance when in one season he transformed the company into baseball players good enough to challenge the men and women of an American air base in nearby Petersfield. It was this energy and perseverance that eventually made his vision of Shakespeare's Globe Theatre, rebuilt on its original site, not a museum, but a working theatre.

Cassio, the aristocratic young lieutenant, was played by Albert Finney, a twenty-two-year-old Lancashire lad, son of a bookmaker, from Salford. Charles Laughton, who was almost sixty, took a great interest in Albert because he was from the North, a little chubby, very talented, and beautiful in a way Charles had never been. I think Charles felt, somewhat vicariously, that he could play roles that he had never played—Romeo, Hamlet, Henry V—through Albert. This is something older actors sometimes do and it does not help either the younger or the older actor. There was a danger in Albert on the stage, but like all young actors, he had to make his own mistakes, his way, in order to develop his own talent.

Othello is the story of a great man brought to an animal state by the need of a low-ranking man to have power over his superiors. Othello is a Moor, an honored black warrior, who has done Venice great service. Desdemona is a high-born, strong-willed, young, white Venetian woman who, against all opposition, loves and marries Othello and moves to the island of Cyprus with her general and his men to defeat the Ottoman fleet. Cyprus is a small island for such tumultuous emotions.

Robeson couldn't have had a more beautiful, feminine Desdemona. Mary Ure made even me desire her. She wore soft leathers, wools, furs (this was 1959, remember), had white blond hair and red, red lips. She smoked Balkan Soubranies, pastel not black, and her perfume was gentle. She lived in a big house in Stratford with Tony Richardson as her brother, guardian, and whatever she wished him to be. They didn't much mix with the company, which was bright of them, because it kept their house a mystery and made us able to imagine all sorts of bacchanalian adventures.

Angela Baddeley, wife of Glen Byam Shaw, played Emilia, wife of Iago and lady-in-waiting to Desdemona, while I was Bianca, Cassio's girlfriend. We also had four great danes, six doves, a monkey, and a whippet. So Cassio's cry "Oh let the heavens give him defense against the elements" on arriving at Cyprus in a great storm, worried about Othello's safety, became "Oh let the heavens give him defense against the elephants!"

While he had been in New York with the then revolutionary *Look Back in Anger*, Tony Richardson became fascinated with improvisation and used it often in the *Othello* rehearsals. It doesn't work in Shakespeare because there is no subtext—just text. Get it right and the emotions will be there. I remember one prime example when Tony asked Paul and Sam to improvise the first jealousy scene. Sam came on at a different place, moved to different places on the stage, and spoke his own lines. Paul came on exactly where he had been set, moved to the places he had rehearsed, spoke Shakespeare's lines exactly, except he prefaced each line with "Jesus Christ, man." End of improvisation. Paul always rehearsed in a dark worsted suit with a knitted vest under his jacket, wearing a dark gray fedora to keep his head warm. He had been seriously ill with pneumonia and could not be chilled—like me when I was a kid with the thermagene vests.

I learned that Paul had played Othello in New York with Uta Hagen in 1945 and in London with Peggy Ashcroft as Desdemona. He had had enormous success in the role, so there wasn't a lot for him to explore, but just his presence and his voice were enough for me.

Dame Edith Evans, the legendary English actress, who had been a milliner until the age of twenty-four, then burst onto the stage and illuminated the theatre for sixty more years. Dame Edith, who would play the Countess of

Rousillon in *All's Well That Ends Well*, was the third member of the company with a boss eye. She didn't hide it. She used it, as she used everything. Her energy was renowned. John Gielgud once said, "Edith's energy is not too much trouble as long as someone throws a bone for her to retrieve for an hour before rehearsal." She was a Christian Scientist, which I believe gave her an antenna that alerted her to anything false. She was hardly beautiful, but could become the most beautiful and desirable woman in the world when the part required it. In life she was not particularly generous, but while playing, she gave her entire self. She was a sensual actress because all her senses were alive to the moment, and thus whatever she encountered was conveyed to the audience. When she touched silk, an audience felt silk. If it was burlap, they felt burlap, and if it was a clammy hand, that is what the audience felt. Her handling of the language was fearless. Her handling of clothes astounded me. I never missed watching Dame Edith's first entrance in *All's Well*, for her train followed her across the stage and curled itself around her feet. Perhaps you have to be a Christian Scientist to achieve this because I have tried and it never works.

All's Well was directed by the great Tyrone Guthrie. There was no love lost between Dame Edith and Guthrie. She was a star. He was not a fan of stars, and Edith didn't need him to be. She never balked at any direction he gave her. If she didn't like it, she just let it get lost.

The play is the story of a brilliant young woman, daughter of a now dead doctor, outside the sphere of regular orthodox physicians who miraculously cures the King of a near fatal disease. She is hopelessly in love with Count Bertram, a spoiled young aristocrat whom nobody loves, except his mother, the Countess of Rousillon. The King gives a great ball to honor Helena and in a misguided moment insists Bertram take Helena for his wife. Bertram is enraged at being given in marriage to a doctor's daughter whom he doesn't love and flies off to Italy as General of Horse to fight bravely in the war. Helena follows him and persuades a pretty young woman who is sleeping with Bertram to let Helena take her place in bed for one night, showing that a young woman scorned is not necessarily powerless. The Countess is very supportive of Helena, as Dame Edith was very supportive of me. I don't think out of the goodness of her heart but because this was what was required for her Countess. An actress takes from the world around her to make a world for her character. The trouble is that theatre is a transient business, so civilians must be wary.

Tyrone Guthrie, a six-foot-five Irishman of noble birth and wicked wit, admired *All's Well* and had previously opened Stratford, Ontario, in that beautiful tent, which he and Tanya Moiseiwitsch had designed, with the same production but Helena was played by Irene Worth, and the King by Alec Guinness.

During rehearsals it was discovered that I had only five seconds to change from my long black woolen dress into my beautiful white ball gown. Guthrie swiftly wrote a scene between two officers in regimental dress that was as Shakespearean as anything else in the play. Tony Guthrie was a pathfinder. He cut a path through the forest and all you had to do was follow it. I never had such an easy time with a part.

Tanya designed an immaculate production, which allowed the men to wear military regimental costumes for formal occasions and khaki shorts, shirts, and berets for daily living. Then of course there were Edith's trains, the white ball gown and a beige linen traveling outfit with a large straw hat that I wore when I went traveling to catch my Bertram, and the most glorious golden pregnancy gown for my return for the end of the play.

Dame Edith got to the theatre three hours ahead of curtain up but her door was closed so her preparations remained a mystery. However, I did see her stand before each performance at the side of the stage with her hands held above her shoulders, shaking them as in a dance of welcome to the gods. "Oh no," she laughed, when I told her what I thought she was doing. "I am simply draining the blood from my hands to make them as slim and white as possible. You should do it."

I didn't watch Dame Edith like a hawk. I didn't need to, we just played together. There was no other way. Her total concentration and belief in the reality of the moment made the reality mine too. It was a huge night for me, that opening night of *All's Well*, my first major exposure in England, and I was rightly terrified. "Oh why?" asked Dame Edith. "You have the next night and the next night and many, many nights to get it right." And I did.

When we were not at the theatre, our little house at Elms Farm, Tiddington, was humming with excitement. I had just opened my play and Mavis, my fellow elf, was to start rehearsals for hers. She was to play the first fairy in Peter Hall's production of *A Midsummer Night's Dream*. Although the first fairy has only one speech and is usually played by a young actor, Mavis had been told over Glen's sherry that Peter wanted her to be a tiny, old first fairy who knitted. The whole company knew how important this was to Mavis because she had never had a part in the three years of walking on; and because they loved her they joined in her excitement. She would talk endlessly about what she would do and how she would do it and I would say crass things like, "Oh Mavis, your first fairy will be the talk of the season!" Then the ax fell. Peter Hall had a change of mind and started bringing endless tap-dancing kids from Birmingham who would stand onstage and say in their Birmingham accents, "Thorough bush, thorough brier," all this to be seen by whomever passed. The company went silent.

Eventually, I was called to Glen's office and told that Peter wanted me to play the first fairy. "Tough," I said. "I won't do it."

"But you must because of your contract."

I hadn't looked at my contract and I didn't have an agent.

"Here," said Glen, "Eighteen pounds, middle billing, and play and understudy as required."

"Glen, this is Mavis's whole season. Is there nothing I can do?"

"Nothing."

"Then let Peter Hall go and live at Elms Farm with Mavis and see what it's doing to her!"

I jumped on my bike and rode to the old Water Mill, where Dame Edith had an apartment. I was repulsive, sobbing, angry, and prepared to kick. Dame Edith gave me a handkerchief and a glass of water, and made me sit down. She said, "You have built a brick wall, which you are beating at with your hands and kicking at with your feet. You are bruised and bloodied and most unattractive. Now, you must take down the wall brick by brick, until you can see over it, and brick by brick until you can, with grace, step over it. Now off you go and be the best first fairy you can be." And I did. But I have never forgiven Peter Hall and I never will.

I have seen two memorable productions of *A Midsummer Night's Dream*—Peter Hall's production that Stratford year and Peter Brook's production eleven years later. Hall's production was set in the time of Elizabeth I, but the humans wore cloth and the fairies made their Elizabethan clothes of thistledown and cobwebs. The effect was truly dreamlike. Brook's production was set in three sides of what could be a squash court, festooned with trampolines and other circus equipment. The effect was startling but the main difference was the incredible clarity of the play. I had never heard and understood every syllable of the text before, and it was shocking to sit in an audience and never for a moment have your attention wander. I remember feeling a breeze around my neck, and I realized that it was because my head had sat high on my spine, as a child's does at a circus, for the entire evening.

All the actors in both productions were the best you

could see anywhere at any time, but Charles Laughton, who had come to play Lear, was born to play Bottom. The unathletic body, the scruffy beard he had grown for Lear and colored ginger for Bottom, his sad, large eyes, and his comic timing, so easy and unforced, made Bottom the Weaver endearing in his boastfulness. His awaking after his night of love with Titania was so full of wonder and a certain gratefulness for such a night. Of course, he had a right to be grateful. He had just spent the night with the Queen of the Fairies in the person of Mary Ure. The strange thing about Mary was that, although she was a practical Scottish woman, she always gave the impression that her feet did not touch the ground.

Lila De Nobili did not give Bottom an ass's head, as is usually done. Charles was given long silky ears and two cloven hooves on his hands, but in front of our eyes, he instantly became an ass and we were allowed to see all the emotions usually hidden.

A Midsummer Night's Dream was written to be performed at the wedding of the Countess of Southampton and her second husband, Sir Thomas Heneage. They, like Duke Theseus and Queen Hippolyta, were not young, but it is a young magical play showing the power and wisdom of the "little people." It is a play full of country folklore put in Shakespeare's head as a child in Warwickshire. This folklore trickles down in the New England of Hawthorne or in the South of Faulkner, Flannery O'Connor, or Eudora Welty, as well as through folk songs of the Appalachians or the hillbilly people of Kentucky today. There is a photograph of our production, and everyone looks wonderful—except one angry first fairy.

There was a trinity of great actors in England for nearly three quarters of a century—Ralph Richardson, John Gielgud, and Laurence Olivier, each idiosyncratically different from the others. Young actors of our generation, therefore, had a wealth of material to admire, copy, and discard, and I always found it fascinating to try to discover the actor who had the greatest influence on them.

Olivier was clearly the most ambitious, the most daring, and the most skilled at creating fireworks. Of the three, he was also the most handsome, but somehow you rarely saw his good looks, which were too often hidden by various noses, teeth, and beards. He rarely revealed himself. He was at home in film as well as theatre, both as an actor and a director. His film of *Henry V*, in which he both directed and starred, is legendary. He had come to Stratford to play Coriolanus. I remember his arrival at the theatre.

The first thing he did was check the crew. He knew their names, the wives' names, and sometimes the names of the kids. He remembered an illness or a marriage. It was a reunion with Uncle Larry, and they would protect him with their lives. Smart move? I don't care, but it was the only time it happened. Then to business. Truthfully, Olivier was a little old for Coriolanus, but it didn't matter a bit. He had carved the part out for himself in a way we younger actors didn't do. His Roman wig, makeup, and costume gave the illusion of youth and virility. He was a brilliant technician but I was searching for something else. Although I marveled at him, I didn't study him.

I knew that Coriolanus is a young patrician admired for his brilliance and bravery in battle. Having saved Rome from the Volsces at Coriole, he is persuaded while at the peak of his popularity to run for public office. Unfortunately, he is not a politician and does not treat the voters decently. As a great war hero he feels he has the right to tell the people of Rome how inferior he feels they are, and he offends them in his speeches. Nearly everyone knows that is not the way to get elected. He is driven from Rome into exile and service with the Volsces. He brings the Volscian army to the gates of Rome and plans to overtake it. Roman senators, patricians, and soldiers come to his tent to beseech him change his mind, all to no avail. He boasts to the Volscian general Aufidius that nothing can dissuade him.

Coriolanus's mother, Volumnia, a great Roman matri-arch who had instilled in her one glorious son the pride and intolerance that he was now displaying, comes to his tent to beg on her knees that he forget his pride and spare Rome. It is a scene that has been played and will be replayed by mothers and sons all around the world—that of a mother trying to persuade a son to relinquish the very things she has taught him and that will now bring about his ruin and the ruin of his family. Each time Dame Edith called Olivier son, my heart broke. Shakes-peare has her say it three times. The word *son* is used so often in life—to the paper boy, to someone you want to lord power over, but when a mother says "son" to her boy, you know they have shared an umbilical cord. Edith Evans, who had never had a child, knew that in her veins.

In 1922 a wise young artist, Boris Aronson, left Russia for America and eventually became one of the foremost designers in New York. He always said he left Russia when they started giving out buttons, little memorial buttons that are pinned onto your coat or dress *everywhere* you go. Boris and his beautiful wife, Lisa, had come to Stratford and made a sculptured set that was exciting to look at and provided Olivier with a *coup de théâtre* at the end of the play.

Standing on top and right at the edge of a cavernous

opening eight feet from the ground, Coriolanus suddenly fell to his death. Of course, he didn't really. Two stalwart young walk-ons held on to his feet, releasing the pressure at a given signal, enabling Coriolanus to begin a fall, which was stopped by their hold on his ankles. There was one deeply dangerous moment when the men released his ankles so he could turn and be facing front as he fell. There he was upside down, swinging back and forth until Aufidius stabbed him repeatedly. In our production, Coriolanus's body was left like Mussolini's to rot.

It was an extraordinary athletic feat for any actor at any age, but the audience expected no less from Olivier and he never let them down. He never missed a perform-ance either. Everyone in the theatre knew it so his under-study, Albert Finney, didn't bother to learn the lines.

We knew that Olivier was simultaneously playing Archie Rice, who is the main character in John Osborne's *The Entertainer*. Archie is a sleazy vaudevillian playing out his life in a seedy seaside resort, laughing and tap-dancing his way into oblivion. The film was being shot in Morecambe, and Olivier was being driven from Morecambe to Stratford and back, getting his rest in the car. A massively demanding task, which only he would be up to.

One night, I was sitting at the side of the stage during

Midsummer Night's Dream watching Mary and Charles, when a white-faced Albert Finney with a rotten cold whispered to me, "Larry has done his knee in, tap-dancing as Archie. He's off tomorrow's matinée and I have to play. Will you help me learn the lines?"

I first put Albert's head over a steaming bowl of eucalyptus and covered him with a towel, to get rid of his cold and clear his brain. We stayed up all night and morning, learning lines until he had to go to the theatre for costume fitting and rehearsal. This is the reason I am so familiar with *Coriolanus*.

Fortunately, Albert's brain was young, as well as cleared, and he learned the part and played marvelously. Being young, he brought things to *Coriolanus* that Olivier couldn't, but without that incredible map that Olivier had already drawn, Albert couldn't have found his way. It is possible to chart a part so that always you know where you are and how much energy will be needed for the next part of the journey.

Dame Edith's Volumnia was definitive, which means I will never play Volumnia. When I have seen an actress totally define a role, I am satisfied and don't need to play it. Volumnia was one, Maggie Smith's Millamant in Congreve's *The Way of the World* was another, while Elizabeth Spriggs's Gertrude in *Hamlet* was a third. It is as though the part is seared into my mind with them and I would only remember and copy.

Most great actors are imitated often because of the voice, which is unlike any other. Dame Edith, John Gielgud, Marlon Brando, Ralph Richardson, and Maggie Smith are all imitated, but because the voice is only part of the whole, it never satisfies and sometime leads us to think that that was all there was. If you look at three films, *Tom Jones*, *The Queen of Spades*, and *Look Back in Anger*, you will see Dame Edith using the same voice but becoming three vastly different human beings.

Charles Laughton had studied the role of Lear for forty years, and intellectually, emotionally, he was ready. But physically he was not. To play any of the great roles, you have to train your body until it is fit enough to do whatever is required of it. Energy, too, is essential. Charles's body was not ready. He was grossly overweight and standing was a chore. He loved to sit on a chair at the center of a circle surrounded by young people sitting or kneeling, listening to his wisdom, and every now and then, it was wisdom, but I am not a great one for sitting and kneeling at anyone's feet. I never have been, and as sitting and kneeling become more difficult with age, I guess I won't ever be. And I don't require it of others younger than I. Charles didn't like me and I didn't much like him, so there was a tension between us, which was good for the play.

Lear has three daughters, two by his first wife, and Cordelia by his second wife. The two older girls, Goneril and Regan, will do anything and say anything to be in their father's good graces. He is the king and is just about to divide and give away his kingdom to his daughters, who will then take care of him for the rest of his life. He convenes a large meeting at which each sibling will say publicly how much she loves him. Goneril speaks first and tells the world how much she loves and reveres her father. Regan goes even further, saying her father means more to her than life itself. Cordelia, who truly loves her father, will say nothing, which so enrages Lear that he disinherits her of all land. She accepts the hand of the King of France and leaves England. The rest of the play shows us the folly of an old, frail man giving away all his power. After scenes of unbearable cruelty and abuse inflicted on him by his two "loving" daughters, Lear and Cordelia are reconciled for a short while before her death.

The actual friction that existed between Charles and me created a live wire, which made the relationship between Lear and Cordelia a real danger zone, as is often the case between parent and favorite child. Unlike Lear and Cordelia, we were never reconciled, but I watched him carefully through rehearsals and every night he played, because in each performance he played one scene definitively. But only *one*, and it was never the same one, so you had to be there all the time. Charles had left out the large ingredient for the big roles—stamina. I felt sad for him as I watched him from the wings. He had come to play Lear and was a memorable Bottom. He never knew of my presence in the wings and I didn't want him to. He taught me a great deal and I am grateful—so grateful that the night before a performance of *Lear*, I took a lot of laxatives to purge myself in order to be as light as possible for him to carry onstage crying, "Howl, howl, howl, howl" at the end of the play.

I did, however, break one of my rules during that season. I had an explosive affair with an actor in the company, causing a lot of havoc and pain, for which I apologize.

Without question, the 1959 season had made a great impression on me. It had stretched me. I had seen great acting and been given the chance to play with great actors and also the chance to play great roles. This time I was a stronger and wiser actress.

− 16 −

London

SWINGING London. Exploding London would be truer to the mark. Since perhaps the Boer War, there had not been a social revolution except for a brief movement in the 1920s. Three great wars had demanded young men of eighteen to be drafted, who were told what to do, how to do it, and where. From 1950 on, however, they were suddenly more free, and that freedom produced the knowledge that they could challenge and break apart the old, creating their own new world in the process.

Three bright young men from Cambridge and Oxford got together and made three short documentary films. Tony Richardson's, *Momma Don't Allow*; Karel Reisz's, *We Are the Lambeth Boys*; and Lindsay Anderson's, *Every Day*

Except Christmas. They were about to transform the face of British film.

Richardson's documentary, the first of these films, was made in 1955. The following year, John Osborne's *Look Back in Anger* erupted at the Royal Court under the true, revolutionary eye of George Devine, with three young actors, Kenneth Haigh, Mary Ure, and Alan Bates, who were directed by Tony Richardson. This production radically changed the way things had been done, and never again would they be what they used to be.

Working-class themes increasingly came to dominate much of the avant-garde of the 1950s. Whereas the 1930s and 1940s had witnessed the glory of the Empire and the courageous men and women who had suffered and fought in the wars, the 1950s and the works of Osborne reflected both anger and derision. This was a new kind of writing without a basic respect for the past. All those traditions, which had taken so many years to form, were apparently not worth anything anymore. Young people always throw away the values of their elders to leave the way clear for the formation of their wisdom, which, when it becomes tradition, will be stomped upon by the next generation. But this new theatre demanded a new kind of actor, less elegant in dress and speech, working class and regional with a new virility, much as the Group Theatre in the 1930s in America consciously set out to form a new kind of acting, one that reflected its generation's own rebellion.

History tells us that revolutions are almost never started by the working class. All too often they are engaged in a form of work that prevents them from initiating radical ideas. It is the privileged intellectual who has the time and energy to sit around making manifestos. And so it was in England.

Meanwhile, I, the daughter of a working-class man, was doing good establishment things for the BBC, productions like *Rogue Herries* by Hugh Walpole and *Justice* by John Galsworthy. Then, Tony Richardson asked me to play the madhouse keeper's wife in Thomas Middleton and William Rowley's *The Changeling* at the Royal Court, which I did, marvelously. While still at the Royal Court, I played Ismene to Mary Ure's Antigone in *Trials by Logue*, as in Christopher Logue, directed by Lindsay Anderson, and sang a song of Johnny Dankworth's, "Open Belly, Open Purse," as a streetwalker.

The father of all this new work, George Devine, asked me to stay on and act in two plays by Eugène Ionesco, a small, round, drunken man who was the king of the theatre of the absurd. He came to London with his tiny

Parisian wife to see Devine's production. I played what Ionesco wrote but I never understood it. I don't think the audience did either.

I was working full-time, but I never felt that I really belonged. The differences between Australia and England proved enormous. The directors, playwrights, and actors of the "We've never had it so good" era had been here in England growing up when the war was raging, whereas I was in Australia sending bundles to Britain, trying to knit balaclavas and tap dancing. Their energy came from the breaking of class barriers. They were talented, powerful, and sexy, but I could not become one of them. I had become what Elsie had wanted me to become, a successful classical young leading lady just as it was going out of style, somehow mirroring the fate of the old British Empire, which was also going out of style. Territorially, the Empire had virtually ceased to be with the independence of India in 1947, followed by a host of other countries breaking free from England's domination. The creative world responded to this revolution with a turbulence all its own. Nobody wanted to be a lord or a knight or a dame anymore; everybody wanted to be working class. John Osborne, Arnold Wesker, John Arden, Harold Pinter, David Storey, and Joan Littlewood were happy revolutionaries and the work they produced was, as they said, alive. They said, "Come in. The water's wonderful."

But I responded, "I can't swim."

Some psychological disorder? Or did I know deep down that England was not where I belonged?

Just as I had longed to get to England, I now longed to get away. I needed a rebirth and Stratford, Ontario, gave it to me. Michael Langham, the director of Stratford in Canada, rang me in the middle of the night in February 1961 to ask how soon could I come to Canada to play Rosaline in *Love's Labour's Lost*. I had never read or seen the play and didn't know who Rosaline was. I asked, "Who got sick?"

"Toby Robbins is pregnant."

"Poor little thing. I must knit her something. Sure I'll come. When?"

"By the end of the week. John Hayes, our general manager, will ring you right back about salary and travel."

I thought, they must do all their business at night to save on cheaper rates. John Hayes did ring right back, and expecting a great deal of bargaining, offered me three hundred dollars.

"Sure" I said. "Send the ticket."

Each time my life seems to have come to a dead end, I

am saved by work. Work in a new place and with new people. I have always felt that a skin begins to grow around your spirit if you are not challenged. If that skin becomes too thick, you're old. I was not going to allow this to become my fate.

~ 17 ~

Stratford, Ontario

I HAD NO idea who anyone would be or how many "soloquies" Rosaline had, but I eagerly flew into Toronto. I was driven to Stratford, agreed to the apartment they had found me, learned that Toby Robbins was the most beautiful woman in Canada, had a rich husband, and didn't need my booties. I quickly bought an old Chevy because I realized that you had to have a car in North America for your independence. The first things I noticed were how large the cars were, how big the country was, and how well-stocked something called Loblaws, a supermarket, was.

There was also a strange way of buying liquor, which you bought from the Ontario Liquor Control Board, housed in Stratford in a plain beige building. No bottles on display and no advertisements. You wrote your order on a sort of laundry list form, gave it to a man in a gray dust coat, who then went down the aisles behind the counter where all the bottles were stacked. He came back with your order in a brown paper bag. You paid, got your liquor, and, presumably, rushed it home and drank it.

I had been brought up in Australia to witness the "six o'clock swill." Pubs were open all day and closed promptly at six. That meant men who had worked all day and were now hot and tired rushed to the bars and, on empty stomachs, gulped down ice-cold, highly alcoholic beer. At closing time, they bought the wife some gladioli and a crayfish, threw up, and went home. If all those restrictions were meant to curb drinking, they sure didn't work, in either country.

Once I was settled, the publicity department of Stratford had asked me to drive to Toronto to appear on a television program about the upcoming season. I was so eager to see more of this big new country that I willingly agreed. The other guests on the program were the three strippers from a production of *Gypsy*, which was playing at the O'Keefe Centre, a gargantuan auditorium at the bottom of Younge Street, the longest street in Toronto. After the interview, I jumped in the Chevy, drove to the theatre, bought my ticket, and realized that I had no money for food. But maybe Ethel Merman's phrasing would make up for that. Working my way to the back row of the balcony mezzanine, I politely declined all the ushers' offers of programs. In England, you pay extra for your programs and I didn't have any extra after paying to park my car. The poor person sitting beside me was bedeviled by my trying to look over her shoulder at her program. She, at last, requested that I ask the usher for a program of my own, but knowing I couldn't afford it, I said, "Oh, no!"

She must have thought I belonged to some strange cult, for I still looked over her shoulder. Ethel Merman from that far back in the theatre looked tiny but packed the same punch as on the screen at the Regent on Collins Street back in Melbourne and had the same marvelous phrasing.

Three weeks after my arrival in Stratford, there was a loud knock on my door. Eight A.M., that's too early I thought, looking at my clock. It had better be important.

It was. It was the sheriff, a gentle, plump man in uniform, who took off his hat, called me ma'am, and handed me an envelope.

"What is this, officer?"

"Divorce papers, ma'am."

"Divorce papers? I'm not even married."

"No, ma'am, you are the corespondent."

"I'm not even a correspondent," I replied, and told him of my learning disability, which made writing difficult. We could have had a fine time on the porch, bantering and laughing, but I decided to open the large official envelope. There in the right-hand corner, was a wonderful photograph of *me*, nine months pregnant.

"Oh, that's not me, that's *Helena*," I said insouciantly. "You see, officer, *All's Well That Ends Well* ends with Helena arriving to confront Bertram, who is unaware that he has made love to her because she tricked him by pretending to be someone else. But they are married and she arrives at the King's reception nine months pregnant and Tanya had given her the most glorious golden gown and obviously someone with humor has drawn up these papers."

The sheriff appeared flustered. He put on his hat and took two steps back. Then I stopped talking, for I read (in that uniquely official print of legal papers) that the respondent, Albert Finney, and the corespondent, Zoe Caldwell, had cohabited at Elms Farm, Tiddington. I didn't have to appear in court. It was never in the papers, so I got on with my Stratford life.

Apart from the great trinity of Richardson, Gielgud, and Olivier, there was one younger actor whom nobody tried to imitate. It was impossible because Paul Scofield had such a secret self that let no one in except his wife, Joy. When I heard he was to play Coriolanus here in Canada, I thought, I can help him with his lines. He also played Don Adriano de Armado in *Love's Labour's Lost*, so there is another role I will never have to play or wish to see anyone else play. His dilapidated Spanish don was of such exquisite sensitivities that he could not bear to bring his gaze upon lesser mortals except one, Jaquenetta, the most slovenly peasant in town.

Rehearsals began and I was stunned to hear Canadian accents sounding so truly Shakespearean, like that of Farmer Goodall. I was suddenly greeted by pronounced *r*'s, short *a*'s, full *o*'s, as well as a new sound, "aboot," as about. The actors were marvelous and I felt at home. I guess we were all colonials. They drank a lot of alcohol but nobody fell over. There was, however, one actress I couldn't take my eyes from. She played Katharine in *Henry VIII*, and without doing anything, captured your emotions. She was clearly of royal birth.

As it turned out, I was wrong because as soon as she played Jaquenetta in *Love's Labour's Lost*, I realized she was of low peasant stock. In fact, she was born of a good upper-class Canadian family, one that had a lot of drunken genes. Her name was Kate Reid, and she was one of the great actresses because she always revealed the humanity of the character she played. I never saw her play Chekhov. I wish I had, for I know I would have learned a lot. I still wouldn't be able to play Chekhov, but I would have bene-fited greatly.

Unlike me, Kate arrived at the theatre each night just at the half hour, having had a great dinner and several martinis. She would visit dressing rooms, dress, walk onto the stage, and she was immediately her character. It took me a lot more time to do all my preparation, which involved stripping away all that belonged to me, and gradually, with makeup, clothes, and hair, layering my character upon me. Then I could gossip with Joy Parker, Paul's wife, who played the Princess of France in *Love's Labour's Lost* and shared my dressing room, and walk onto the stage as myself playing a character, sometimes marvelously, sometimes not.

There is a strange lightness and freedom when you are playing well. Of course, we all aim for this, but no matter how many rituals you go through, the theatre gods have your performance in their hands. That is why I do not understand actors who insist on only playing five or six performances a week, because only then will they be able to give their best performances. There is no way of knowing which performance will be your best. Only if it has been filmed and set forever can you know.

I didn't get to know Kate Reid that season, but later she became a close friend and it broke my heart to see her broken down by liquor and cigarettes.

I did, however, get to know Joyce Smith from Jamaica. Australia still had the White Australia Policy as I was growing up, which meant I saw Aborigines in the outback from a train window and the Katherine Dunham dancers, at the Princess Theatre, when I was a little girl, but no other blacks. Mum and I always stood at the stage door after any performance, never to speak or ask for an autograph or intrude on the performer's privacy, but just to look. And outside the Princess Theatre on the night the Katherine Dunham dancers performed, I could not stop looking. Everything about these performers was exotic and I, as a ten-year-old girl, longed to be able to be close and touch their hair. Children always want to touch and smell and, sometimes, explore with their mouths things that are unknown to them. They should be allowed such exploration, because it is a human response to look, touch, taste, and smell. Our senses enable us to learn and understand and not be afraid of the unfamiliar. My need to know through my senses is strong, but sometimes I need to know so badly that I avert my eyes and move on and remain afraid. Also, knowing how our native black Australians had been treated in their own country by white Australians made that fear mix with guilt—two senses that do not lead to easy acquaintance.

Joyce, who was slim and pretty, had come to Canada to be nurse, companion, and total caregiver for a woman badly crippled by poliomyelitis. Joyce had to be with her twenty-four hours a day to feed, bathe, turn her in bed, give her a bedpan, and entertain her. The woman was in her middle forties while Joyce was eighteen. She was given records to dance to and pretty clothes to wear, just as long as she was never out of reach.

My tiny apartment was in the house belonging to the woman. Because I saw the strain that each of them was under, I kept my door open during the day, and if Joyce had five minutes, she would come in, whether I was there or not, and be an eighteen-year-old girl. I would tell her news of the theatre, sometimes of the world, and we would laugh and talk of her life in Jamaica and mine in Australia. She let me touch her hair and her skin, and examine the line where her dark skin stopped and the pink palm of her hand began. I think we both learned about each other until color disappeared and we were just two people who could like or dislike one another. I needed that.

I also needed my privacy. Perhaps that need stemmed from my early life behind those iron railings in Moir Street. However, that is difficult to come by when you are part of a big company. Parties are not my idea of heaven, but you must go and have a drink and a dance or two or you seem a bit of a recluse. While at the theatre, I am totally involved but I need to escape after the performance. The world sees actors as constantly "at it like knives," staying up all night. If it were true, we would all look so tired on the stage. Some actors can dance the night away and I'm grateful, for it keeps alive the aura of glamour. I have never played two consecutive seasons in the same place after Stratford-upon-Avon, and I always tried to find an Elms Farm away from town.

I soon realized that I really liked Canada and I liked Canadians. When the season ended, I, being a gypsy, went where the work was, which was Toronto. Canadian television at the time was first-rate and very daring. The directors had been cameramen, and I trusted the cameramen totally. Paul Almond asked me to play Lady Macbeth opposite Sean Connery. It was a low time for Sean. He was a splendid actor but his wife, Diane Cilento, was a shining star. He came with a cold, hung on to it all through rehearsals, and he couldn't learn the lines. I was sharing an apartment with my old friend Judy Wright, who now lived in Canada, and we decided to help Sean. He is a generous man, bright with great humor, which dimmed a little when he had his head over a bowl of steaming eucalyptus covered by a towel. Well, it worked again. With a clear head, he learned his lines and was, not surprisingly, a fine Macbeth. Why shouldn't he be? He is a man, a Scot, and a Shakespearean actor.

What truly stuns me is the daring way Shakespeare presents Macbeth not as an evil man but a man who, while we are watching, removes himself from all human contact. "Laugh to scorn the power of man" sends chills up my spine, for if that advice is followed, a man will surely become alone and powerless.

There was something touching about the way Sean would glance at me, as if at Lady Macbeth, if he were a little unsure of a line. Good for the play. Then off he went to New York to speak to some film men about the possibility of his playing some fellah named Bond, James Bond.

I did all sorts of marvelous plays for the Canadian Broadcasting Corporation: Shaw's *The Apple Cart* (Orinthia), *The Lady's Not for Burning* (Jennet, in my own voice), and some fine new Canadian plays. In the coldest part of the year, I flew to Winnipeg and the Manitoba

Theatre Centre with Douglas Rain as Christy Mahon in J. M. Synge's *The Playboy of the Western World*, and I played Pegeen Mike as well as I could.

Canada, in fact, transformed me. It gave me a new part of the world to explore and time to think about my life as a woman on her own with money enough, plenty of work, good new friends, but with a strange yearning to go back to my roots. I'm not very good at making things happen, in life or in the theatre, but when things do happen, I take up the challenge and thrive.

~ 18 ~

Back to Fowler's

THE AUSTRALIAN government had sent me away five years before to learn all I could learn and bring that knowledge home. The Australian Elizabethan Theatre Trust now invited me to come home to play the title role in *Saint Joan*. I thought this would be interesting since I would be playing it with an Australian company. I was flown home, first class, to meet the director, a truly nice middle-aged professor from the University of San Francisco. There were Australians in the company of course, but not enough. I suddenly realized how chauvinistically Australian I was. Well, Joan was chauvinistically French. However, if I was to lead the company, I must parent it. The closest I could come to that was by being a young rebellious aunty.

There is not a lot of research to do when it comes to Joan. Shaw was very clear about what he wanted, almost too clear. He is like Eugene O'Neill in that respect. You can almost play it with Shaw as the director. There is a little book about the historical Joan with transcripts of the trial that stunned me. The really great Shavian lines are not Shaw's but Joan's own lines, which make her an extraordinarily bright and remarkable creature. It amazes me that people in Australia remember my Saint Joan and recall it as a sort of breakthrough, which is not my own recollection. This is not mock modesty. I just don't understand why. When I act, I want to examine something about the human condition, some frailty that enhances it or makes it clearer, but when I explored Joan, I could not find that chink in her armor. I did, however, believe her voices. The play itself discusses the human condition, creating an argument between the spiritual and the political, but I was Joan, not the audience.

We performed in all the capital cities and in Melbourne we played the Tivoli Theatre, where I had last appeared as Slightly Soiled nearly twenty years before. The stage at the Tivoli was slightly shallower than the other theatres we played, so the long set of steps leading to the cathedral in the play had to have slightly different dimensions. We had only time for a cue-to-cue rehearsal before we opened. (That means you cut from lighting cues to sound cues to entrances and exits. The whole play is not rehearsed.) It was a real "welcome home, Zoe" first night with Mum and Dad in the front row. I was prepared to be brilliant. I believe I was until I dropped to my knees at the top of the cathedral stairs and with my sword held high for God, France, and the Dauphin, I suddenly realized there was no stair under my knees and down, down, down, I went, flat out like a lizard drinking. I thought, well, I've taken this spectacular fall without killing myself. I best remain here and pretend I blacked out in a religious ecstasy. You cannot believe the credit I got for such an inventive piece of stagecraft. Never before had any Joan done that. And I hope no Joan ever will again.

While I was playing in Sydney, Australia's great writer Patrick White and his longtime companion, Manoly Lascaris, came backstage and invited me to dinner. Patrick had written a new play, *The Season at Sarsaparilla,* set in the suburbs with a part, Nola Boyle, I knew I could play. Nola Boyle had a mane of tawny hair and the body of a full-blown woman, and rarely got out of her chenille dressing gown. The "season" referred to the time when the whole street seemed in heat, affecting both humans and dogs. Nola was married to a garbageman and badly wanted children. I badly wanted Nola. Patrick was mightily depressed when he met me after *Saint Joan*. I had dark hair, a basin cut, and was, of course, small.

"Don't worry," I said. "I can be Nola, no sweat." I remembered the parts I wouldn't have played at the Union Theatre Rep if parts had been given to the actor on the basis of size. We had come to the end of the tour, so Patrick asked me to first play a small part in his play *The Ham Funeral*, which was to open in a month in Sydney. I think he was punishing me for not looking like Nola Boyle. He didn't quite understand that actors become who they need to become and how could I play Saint Joan looking like Nola Boyle?

After those months playing *The Ham Funeral*, I ran back to Melbourne to ask Mum's help in becoming Nola. Dad just watched the process and was grateful that we were doing the new play in Adelaide. His furniture was safe.

Mum had a full figure but was always a very meticulous dresser. I loved to watch her from start to finish. She was never seen without a brassiere and corset. And that was what I wanted from her. An old brassiere and corset padded loosely but fully, like flesh that would feel like Nola's body. Mum made all her own clothes and, when I was young, mine too. She worked her pedal Singer sewing machine like a wizard. She needed only one day to give me Nola's body. Now I was after Mum's nightie and light green chenille dressing gown. It was the perfect color, the perfect degree of dilapidation. I needed all three: the body, the nightie, and the chenille dressing gown. Now I was Nola, but only from the neck down. I had seven months growth of hair and had been putting on weight. Now to the hairdresser to become a tawny blonde.

Patrick kept writing to ask how things were going, and because I don't write letters, Mum took up the slack and began what would be, for her, a lifelong correspondence. Patrick White was not always an easy man but Mum and he seemed relaxed with each other. Letters do that, I have learned.

The dyeing took the health out of my hair and with a bit of back-combing it became a mane. The strange thing about being a blonde was that men held doors for me and carried my suitcase. They never had before. Maybe I felt differently and didn't rush to open doors and pick up my suitcase.

Nola Boyle was polar opposite to me. She was fleshy, besides being blond, and didn't have the acting opportunities to cure her longing for love, children, and a good time. The suburb she lived in didn't approve of her. I loved her.

I spent day and night in Nola's body, nightie, and dressing gown so that friends who came to the house were amazed to see how I had let myself go. This is not always necessary but it is the way I work. If my character needs to be thin, I become anorexic; if fat, too fat. I think it is called overacting and it is not good for your body, but it was great for Nola's.

We rehearsed and opened in Adelaide. *The Season at Sarsaparilla* was a great success and I was very good as Nola. I loved her, of course. Patrick was so bowled over by the transformation and so pleased with everything that he and Manoly adopted me. I now had two strict uncles to keep an eye on my affairs both of the heart and the mind. I was lucky. When the play came to Melbourne, to the Union Theatre Rep, Mum asked Patrick whether he would like to stay with them in Balwyn because by this point I was staying at his house whenever I was in Sydney.

Manoly and he had a great Australian house in Sydney, grew their own vegetables and fruit, and kept goats. They had about six pugs. Patrick was from an old Australian family, while Manoly came from a well-born Greek family. They had met in World War II and had been together ever since, a truly great marriage. Patrick came to Melbourne without Manoly because one of them had to take care of the land and the animals. He slept in

Bert's sleepout. Bert had long gone. I still have a photo of Mum and Dad with Patrick in our backyard. They look a funny trio and you would never guess that one of the men would win the Nobel Prize for Literature in 1973.

During *The Ham Funeral,* I had taken up with a thirty-two-year-old guitar maker who was a stagehand at the Theatre Royal in Sydney. He made beautiful guitars and wrote songs for the Labor Party and we made a plan, once acting was out of the way, to go bush. He had an old elegant Riley and was a tall, thin, red-haired Aussie with a true Aussie face and a laconic manner. I had been all around Australia and was treated like an important person. Now I would be just a woman traveling the road with her man. This was important, to try to locate the real Australian in me. I would know what an early Australian woman felt like in the bush with her man. We took a fishing rod, Mum and Dad's tent, two pots and pans, two tin plates, a knife, fork, and spoon each, and two tin mugs. Also the guitar-mending tools, a bush knife, the guitar, and a large sleeping bag. We would live off the land and make enough money for petrol by mending guitars. We would travel all around Australia. Pretty romantic idea with no basis of reality. People who played guitars sure wanted them mended but had no money to pay for the mending. I made a lamb stew that lasted for ten days, breakfast and dinner, by simply adding more flour, more water, and whatever fruit and vegetables we could steal. We did catch fish in the various rivers where we made camp and fried them in fat. We had our little tin billycan for our tea, and as soon as the sun went down, mosquitoes as large as bats. But help was on the way in the form of a cyclone. Cyclone Annie blew our tent away, while we slept, what's more. We had reached Moreton Bay up on the Queensland coast, just north of Brisbane, which unlike Melbourne, was semitropical, and a colony of Aussie Communists generously took us in. The men were merchant seamen, while the women looked after the children, the vegetable growing, the laundry, and the cleaning of the houses. There were guitars to be mended and I would help with the women's chores. It seemed great to me. So we settled in. They were good people who proselytized a bit and sang songs like "Open the Window and Let Peace Fly In" and the fact that I knew Paul Robeson carried weight. But would I live out the rest of my days at Moreton Bay? I sent home for money.

While I was still in this colony, I told the women the story of Aristophanes' *Lysistrata*, which is set in fifth-century B.C. Athens during the time of the Peloponnesian Wars. So many men had been killed, so much money given toward war, and women had more responsibilities.

So one sharp Athenian wife, Lysistrata, persuaded all the Athenian woman to lock themselves in the Acropolis and refuse the men sex until they made peace.

This fascinated the Moreton Bay wives because here were their men sitting around singing songs about peace, while we women were making the fires and grilling the meat. Why not a song for the women to sing? So I wrote one, to the tune of "Oh Tannenbaum," and we women sang, with our strong antipodean accents:

In the golden days of Ancient Greece,
There lived a Ly-sis-tra-tar
Who did believe that to get peace
One must become a mar-tyr
So women all their love withheld
And so to peace were men compelled
The moral of this story ist,
No roots unless we co-exist.

P.S.: Roots is Australian for sexual congress.

It seemed to go down well, but two days later the money arrived and my man and I were traveling home.

Mum waited outside our house in Balwyn, and as soon as the Riley pulled up, she said, "Zoe, you have to ring Sir Tyrone Guthrie." While I had been off being a pioneer woman, Tony Guthrie had written a letter, which Mum naturally had opened, asking me to join a company in Minneapolis that he, Oliver Rea, and Peter Zeisler were starting. The Guthrie Theatre was to be a classical repertory company, an American classical repertory company. And unbeknownst to me, there was a great gnashing of teeth at Actors' Equity that two of the parts should be given to a foreign actress whom they had never heard of. Tony allowed as how thirty-four of the parts were going to Equity members, so surely he could have one foreign actress who had extensive experience in repertory companies. Mum, the writer of the family, answered Tony's letter by saying that I had gone bush to find myself, that she didn't know where I was, but she knew I would soon get in touch and that I would say yes because I loved Minneapolis. Mum had never heard of Minneapolis and neither had I. Tony adored the letter and wrote back. Mum now had two very distinguished pen pals.

Having located the real Australian in me, I was now free and yearning to experience America. The year was 1963. I got my papers in order, bought Mum and Dad their first new car—a Hillman Minx—and flew to Canada to play Jennifer Dubedat in *The Doctor's Dilemma*, for the CBC. Then I flew on to St. Paul, the home of the

Minnesota immigration department, which had given me permission to enter the country as a visitor, a kind of wetback, without a work permit.

Tony Guthrie and his equally tall, equally aristocratic wife, Judy, met me and took me immediately to see the Mississippi River because it was solidly frozen but about to thaw. The same tinkling sounds as the Neva on the other side of the world. Then we were off to a hotel in Minneapolis to brush up for a party in the reception room for all concerned with the new theatre and the new company. I knew nobody except Tony, Judy, and Douglas Campbell, an actor-director who had been at Stratford, Ontario.

New territory, new people, a fresh start, all the things I love. I met Hume Cronyn and his beautiful wife, Jessica Tandy, for the first time, but had no idea how important they would become in my life. I met a beautiful young actress, Ellen Geer, who I was told was the daughter of Will Geer and who had just married Ed Flanders; a great-looking couple, Lee and Elaine Richardson; George Grizzard; John Cromwell and his wife, Ruth Nelson; and a sexy-looking actress named Rita Gam. Robert Pastene must have been there but I didn't notice. There were so many new people, so many new names. Outside the snow was piling up and paths were being shoveled through the roads and sidewalks. This was really new territory.

The day after I arrived, we were scheduled to meet at the theatre, which was mostly a shell, do our Equity duties, and look at designs and sketches for *Hamlet* and *The Miser*. Rehearsals would begin the following day. We had two months to rehearse two plays, get the cement mixers out of the auditorium, cover it with carpet and install the multicolored seats, get to know one another, and open the first big classical repertory company in America. The excitement level was very high, with all hoping they would be good enough for everyone else.

I was immediately given a lesson in humility, since I was asked to leave a meeting between Equity and the company. They would discuss and vote whether I should be given a work permit. I meekly left the room and waited outside. I had an Australian, an English, and a Canadian Equity card.

Did I really need this, I thought.

"No," said Sue Vale. So I went into the meeting and said calmly, "Don't bother voting. I shall leave tomorrow and save you all this trouble."

Hume Cronyn stood up and said, "Miss Caldwell, I must confess that I am a member of the Equity Council who has tried to keep you out. But I want to suggest to my fellow Equity members that you be given a work permit."

I thought, He may be small, but he has power and I think he is my friend.

Hamlet would open the theatre, followed by *The Miser* and, later, *The Three Sisters*. I didn't go to the early rehearsals of *Hamlet*. I tried to find that little house away from everyone, as well as an old car. The car was easy, a black Oldsmobile; the seclusion was not. I took a room at a large house at the summit of the hill up from the theatre and shared a huge kitchen with about eight company members. Our wonderful landlady, Mildred Van Horne, had been a showgirl at the Chicago World's Fair in the 1930s and had parlayed whatever she had, certainly charm and a sweet disposition, into a lot of money. She was now a Brahmin with her own guru. There was to be no alcohol consumed on the premises and no illicit lovemaking or smoking. Nonetheless, our kitchen became the unofficial after-theatre club. Everyone came, everyone drank, some smoked, and everyone ate. Eating was allowed. Our landlady never said a word. I suppose she remembered Chicago.

The first rehearsal of *The Miser* was a terrible dustup. Hume Cronyn had taken the Miles Mallison version to his island in the Bahamas and learned all his lines and worked out the moves only to be given the version that we would do, which was the Richard Wilbur translation. The difference in the two versions was considerable. A whole other world. Miles Mallison, who was a large, gifted comedian, had adapted *The Miser* for his particular talent, while Richard Wilbur, the American poet, had translated a lot of Molière, always in rhyming couplets. His work is pristine and brilliant. We were all dismissed and told to come back the next day. The directors would arbitrate and the final word would be Tony Guthrie's. The next day we read the Wilbur version and started to rehearse.

I quickly realized that all the actors were deferring to Hume. He was a well-known actor playing Harpagon, the title role. But that is not healthy for either side. So when my time came to rehearse Frosine (the matchmaker), I did just what I wanted to do, and quickly Hume and I had a tennis match. If you are a good player, you want to pit yourself against someone better than you. That's what Hume and I did and that is why our scene was so successful with the audience.

Molière took the story of *The Miser* from Plautus and, as he always did, infused it with French wit so that greed, suspicion, avarice, self-interest, and an inability to trust anyone became so funny and ultimately touching. Hume had a triumph as Harpagon.

Before I start rehearsing, I always ask to look at my costume sketch, which is something I recommend to every actor. You would be amazed at how much I learn from doing this. Does her petticoat show, are her hands wearing gloves, are they together, above her head, and is she pointing her toe? Then I try for one second during the performance to look like the sketch. Our costume designer, Tanya Moiseiwitsch, had given Frosine outrageous clothes befitting a woman of intrigue—an enormous straw hat, wonderful purple gloves, many, many petticoats, and lots of exposed shoulders with a large beauty mark on her left breast, which showed up well against the wet white body makeup that I put on every piece of visible skin. My skin is not white, so I had a lot of making up to do. Hume made the beauty spot a comic feature by pretending that it was a large insect that needed removing.

The third play that inaugural season was a new translation of *The Three Sisters* by Leonid Kipnis and Tony Guthrie, and it was during the rehearsals that I realized what a truly splendid company it was. The three sisters, Jessica Tandy (Olga), Rita Gam (Masha), and Ellen Geer (Irina), had come from different points of the compass in every way. Jessica had been a very much admired actress in England as a young woman, then crossed the Atlantic to become a much sought after beauty in America, until Hume captured her and proceeded to make possible roles that she created and illuminated: the original Blanche DuBois in *A Streetcar Named Desire*, opposite Marlon Brando, being the pinnacle. She never left the theatre, grew as an actress until, in her eighties, she was untouchable.

Rita Gam was born to be photographed, and so into the movies she went. Her father and mother were upper-class European Jews and I think that was what Rita drew on to play her Masha. I wish everyone had seen her play it. She was superb.

Ellen Geer had been born and raised in California where her father had an outdoor Shakespeare theatre. She had performed with her mother and sisters singing and playing guitar, and acted with her father, in a company in San Diego. She was beautiful, open, and deeply American. Woody Guthrie had written a song for her when she was a tiny girl.

But the miraculous thing was that, just as Chekhov had written it, they became sisters—the Prozorov sisters.

The other members of the cast included Robert Pastene as Vershinin, Claude Wollman as Toozenbach, George Grizzard as Soliony, Charles Cioffi as Andrey, and

Ruth Nelson as Anfisa. Every single actor seemed wholly in the world of Russia and familiar with one another. Tony didn't play games with them, but let them find each other and the text. He trusted them. But he was bored and Tony could never be bored, so he made me entertain himself and the company by playing Natasha with a Midwest accent and making her loud and repulsive. I felt out of time and not belonging to anyone. Now Natasha is excluded from her first entrance to the party with her provincial little dress with the bright green sash, and the sisters are truly cruel to her, but in this case I thought Tony and I were cruel to her.

My fears were well grounded. The production and all the other actors were rapturously received, while I was torn apart. Rightly so. Edward Payson Call, the stage manager, then gave me a book of Chekhov's letters. Reading them, I realized that although Chekhov reprimanded family, friends, and lovers, he was never gratuitously cruel. Just before Tony left to go back to Ireland to make jam (Tony and Judy Guthrie were the lord and lady of Anna-ma-Kerrig, a very drafty castle in County Monaghan, and because the townspeople were poor the Guthries started a jam-making factory), I told him what I thought. He said, "You're quite right and I know you'll fix it." And I did, but it took me the rest of the season. We so often learn big wisdom from our mistakes. If a director asks of you something that you know is not what the author intended, don't make a fuss—just let it get lost.

When Ellen Geer, wife of Ed Flanders, got pregnant, I was to take over as Ophelia. I needed a third time with her, and with Ellen's help, I put both parts of Ophelia together and was so good that I never have to play her again.

Robert Pastene played Polonius as I have never seen him played before or since. Pastene is a tall, elegant man who for reasons known only to himself, keeps his head on one side. Sometimes more, sometimes less. It doesn't matter because he is one of the best actors in the world. All the equipment is his. He is dangerous, intelligent, articulate, and beautiful, and has a well of sadness to draw from. Wit is his easy companion. He keeps himself away from the big cities of the world and so he will never have a Tony, an Oscar, an agent, or a big bank account, but he will forever have my admiration and respect because I have never seen him play any role that he did not totally define. Young actors should be seeing him.

The season of regional companies is usually nine months, and just as a baby in the womb goes through all the stages of evolving life, so does the actor in a company. But unlike the newborn baby, there comes a dying fall before you leave and a sort of sadness.

But since I've always been a gypsy, I'm prepared to pack my books, records, eiderdown, and bed linen and off I go to the next gig. No one understands why I don't just leave my things there for the next season. Well, I do. That would be taking care of the future and not just living in the present. That's the thing to watch out for in regional theatres: that layer of fat that comes with knowing the certainty of the future. Actors should be a little hungry. It's good for the danger level.

The next job I was offered was a tour with the Canadian Players. They send tours all over Canada, and I was asked to join with William Hutt and two other actors to play *Private Lives* and *Masterpieces of Comedy*, a collection of comic scenes.

Bill was and is Canada's leading actor. One evening during a performance of *Private Lives*, I accidentally tripped him during one of Amanda and Elyot's fight scenes and he came crashing down, breaking his leg. The performance stopped and he was carted off to hospital on a gurney. He played the rest of the tour in a wheelchair, and a great wave of sympathy washed over him everywhere we went, until we played St. Catharines in southwest Ontario. I hit Bill over the head with an old gramophone just as Mr. Coward asks Amanda to do, and the record broke in two as planned but delivered Elyot a cut to the head. You know how a head wound bleeds—all over the stage. I am very fond of Bill Hutt and admire him enormously but so do theatregoers, and I was indeed lucky to get out of St. Catharines alive.

My next lady and my next job was Countess Aurelia, in *The Madwoman of Chaillot* by Jean Giraudoux, at the Goodman Theatre in Chicago. It was while playing there that I became aware that people thought I would never marry. "And you never married, Miss Caldwell?" reporters would ask. In the early sixties, thirty seemed to be the cut-off date. After that you had missed your tram. I was stunned. Of course I would marry and have two children. You had only to read my hand. Still I felt I had better watch it. After Brecht's *Mother Courage and Her Children,* which was my next job, I would really set my mind to it and rustle me up a husband. I suppose it was something that had not been a priority and I suppose it was this dilemma that made me truly sin.

When I returned to the Manitoba Theatre Centre, it was to meet as fine a company of actors as you are likely to find. Francis Hyland, Douglas Rain, William Needles, Martha Henry, Len Cariou . . . in fact, every single actor in every part was superb. John Hirsch, a uniquely gifted man, was to direct the Brecht play. For the first and last time, I did no homework. *Madwoman* closed on a

Saturday night and I flew to Winnipeg on Sunday to begin rehearsals Monday, barely having read the play. Every actor was prepared, except me. I had songs to learn, difficult songs, and a company to head. Of course I couldn't do it. Since I already had a virus, I stood on the corner of Portage and Maine, one of the coldest places, outside Russia, in the world, opened my coat, and let those icy winds blow across the prairies to give me pneumonia. I wouldn't be able to play but I would have the sympathy vote. As it turned out, I did get sicker but the doctor who treated me was a subscriber and wanted to see *Mother Courage.* He put me on cortisone and I went on.

I know I could be a remarkable Mother Courage, that shrewd, tough, stupid, courageous Brechtian rat scurrying and selling her way through the Thirty Years' War, pulling all her possessions, including her children, in that wagon. To protect those possessions, she loses her children and any power that she was born with. I must return to *Mother Courage.* I just wish I could have the same company when I do.

After the Guthrie Theatre's first season a swell little bandit named Peter Witt made himself my agent, but not for the sort of work I was doing. "There is no money in that, darling," he would say, although he was prepared to send me to Los Angeles to audition for a comedy series;

once I had that, I would make acres of money, and I would be able to do whatever I wanted. I wanted to do what I was doing, which was to return to Minneapolis and the Guthrie to play Millamant in *The Way of the World* (I hadn't yet seen Maggie Smith's or I would not have done it), as well as Grusha in *The Caucasian Chalk Circle*. And I did. Mum was right: I did love Minneapolis.

I had just arrived in Minnesota for the 1965 season when I received a letter from Dad telling me that Mum had cancer and would have about two years to live. They must be with me, I thought. Since I must be in Minneapolis, therefore, they must be in Minneapolis.

I rang Mum's doctor and asked him whether it would be safe for her to travel.

He said, "Yes, but it's too long a plane ride. A ship would be better."

So I rang Mum. "Darling, do you think you could manage to come to me in Minneapolis if you sail on a ship?"

There was a long pause.

"Will there be dancing on the ship, Zoe, because if so, I'll need a new evening dress."

They sailed to Hawaii, rested for a week, then sailed to Vancouver, had another week, then caught a train through the Rockies to Minneapolis.

"Oh Mum, I wish you had arrived last week. There was snow up to your ears."

"Oh, Zoe, not in the streets?" Mum didn't understand snow.

That season in Minneapolis I lived in a marvelous eagle's nest on the top of a house on Summit Avenue. The whole top floor with windows all around and a balcony off Mum and Dad's room. They had their own bathroom and a tiny elevator to get them to the ground and back up. I did my usual "I'm only here for the season" decorating, which meant old comfortable couches and chairs from the Salvation Army, with clean, bright, Indian cotton throws. Cinder blocks sat in the middle of the main room supporting a piece of wood six feet in diameter, making a big round table where everyone sat and drank and talked.

I painted the walls, as usual, flat white. I had shopped and shopped so my parents could stay up there away from everyone, except me, until they felt ready.

One Saturday, after rehearsals, Tony Guthrie asked, "So what's the matter with them? Have they each grown an extra head?"

"Come on Sunday with Judy and Tanya, and we'll all have a drink," I suggested.

And they did. They sat around that big round table and talked and drank and laughed until the sun went down. Now my parents were ready to meet the company and join the Minneapolitan life.

Mum and Dad really loved Minneapolis, and the company responded in kind. Mum never complained, although she got tired and looked wan when I sent them on a Greyhound bus to New York. Peter Witt took care of them there, which made me realize the value of an agent. They saw everything that was offered, including *Funny Girl* with Barbra Streisand, and Mum was voted the most popular person on the bus. After seven months they had to fly home and Mum was taken straight to the hospital for major surgery. She had of course kept a diary and gave a lecture on "My Time in America with Zoe."

Before moving on to Minnesota, Tony Guthrie and Tanya had designed the exquisite tent at Stratford, Ontario, which eventually became solid. It is, I think, the most beautiful theatre in North America, inside and out, a true amphitheatre. The wood used for the stage and columns and the subtle colors of the walls and seats all blend harmoniously. They then collaborated with Ralph Rapson in the design of the Guthrie. The Guthrie is purposely off-kilter and full of color and glass windows, and

I always have a sense of excitement walking into it, either from the front of house or from backstage.

Hume and Jess had, like me, skipped a season and were now back leading a company with some old and some new members, but gone was the anxiety of "Will I be good enough for everyone else?" We were full-fledged members of a very special theatre and we knew it. It takes a while for that to happen. Nancy Wickwire, a superior actress, had come to play in *The Way of The World* and Strindberg's *Dance of Death*. The especially dangerous Ed Flanders was back to pit his skill against ours. Maureen Stapleton once said that her favorite actors were "fast" actors—Ed was a fast actor. Ken Ruta was a necessary actor. The company needed him onstage and off. Of course, Robert Pastene was there again, which made me look forward to new revelations in the work.

I know that *The Way of the World* was fine, but *The Dance of Death* with Wickwire and Pastene was world-class theatre. Both actors were tall, both had sexual magnetism, and both had a fierce control. When they walked around each other, you knew that to get between them could mean death. I had seen the play several times but never had I been so mesmerized.

The Cherry Orchard, with Jessica Tandy as Ranyevskaya, was especially lovely, and the season opened with Hume

Cronyn playing *Richard III*, directed by Guthrie, which really kept you awake and in your seats.

The climax of the season for me was *The Caucasian Chalk Circle*, and to do penance for *Mother Courage*, I did all my homework. I also had the perfect director for the Brecht play. Edward Payson Call had paid his dues as stage manager during the early days of Ted Mann's Circle in the Square in Greenwich Village, followed by two years as stage manager at the Guthrie. He had done his homework!

We rehearsed surrounded by huge black-and-white blowups of the mountains of the Caucasus and Caucasian farmer peasants. Ed also brought into the company some American Indians who lived in Minnesota to add to our actors wearing Texas dirt and peasant clothes designed by Lewis Brown. Jessica asked to be part of the villagers, and one day one of the Indian women wondered whether she was the Jessica Tandy who was an actress. Jessica allowed as how she was, to which the woman replied, "I thought so, because you were in my crossword puzzle this morning." Jess was delighted.

I knew I must do two things for Grusha: carry the baby on my back in the proper way and become the closest person in the theatre to the little boy who would play the child. One of the Indian women showed me exactly how to lay the baby in the material on the ground, bundle him with some of the material, then swing the two ends over my head, and when the baby was in the correct part of my back, tie the two ends around my waist. The baby was safe and Grusha had both hands free to climb the mountains. The little boy was seven years old and not one bit arch. He came straight to me and we spent the days of the rehearsals together. We had lunch together, snacks together, and one day he asked his mother if he could have me home for a sleep-over.

The Circle of Chalk is an old Chinese play that examines the principle of ownership. Bertolt Brecht had moved it to the mountains of the Caucasus. Hence, *The Caucasian Chalk Circle*. It tells the story of a young peasant girl who finds an abandoned baby in the wake of the sacking of the Governor's mansion during a revolution. The Governor and his wife are so busy saving their possessions that they have left behind their only son. Grusha takes on the responsibility of caring for the baby and, in spite of hazardous mountains and dangerous bridge crossings, protects and teaches him. When peace is restored, the Governor's wife returns and reclaims the boy, now six. Grusha and she are brought before a wily old judge who will decide which woman is the rightful mother of the boy. He draws a circle of chalk with the boy in the middle and declares whichever woman pulls him out of the circle will take possession of him. The Governor's wife and Grusha each take an arm and pull, but quickly Grusha releases him for fear of harming him. The judge declares the boy hers. Thus, the Communist doctrine is spread. The belief that if you take care of the land, it is yours. That production was one of my best experiences.

About three weeks before the end of the season, two things happened that altered the course of my life. Jessica and Hume had me to dinner to meet Hume's newly widowed cousin, Robert Whitehead. They knew I was longing to marry and have children, and Robert was childless. I met a beautiful, lonely, deeply sad man in mourning, and although we cleaned the dishes very well together, we would not become romantically involved.

The second thing was a phone call from Peter Witt to tell me to come straight to New York from Minneapolis because Anne Bancroft was going to Caneel Bay in the Virgin Islands with her husband, Mel Brooks, for two weeks. And they needed me to help them pack? No. Alexander Cohen, who was the producer of John Whiting's play *The Devils* at the Broadway Theatre, a huge musical house, wanted me to step into the role of Jeanne while Anne was on vacation.

It was directed by Michael Cacoyannis, best known for the film *Zorba the Greek*. Jason Robards was Grandier.

Of course I'd come. It was my next offer. I knew the play and admired it enormously, although I had not played it. I had seen Dorothy Tutin play it in London, but not define it. I would miss the Guthrie, which is now a very vital part of American theatre, and I regard it as my American alma mater. But I packed my records, books, linen, and eiderdown, and drove in my white Corvair Monza to New York.

Part Three

1965–1967

~ 19 ~

My Broadway Debut

ACTING as a replacement was the best possible way for me to make my Broadway debut because nobody knew me except people who had seen me play elsewhere. I had no huge responsibilities, just the normal ones of studying the play and what the playwright wanted, and of keeping the audience awake and in its seats.

Hume and Jess, whom I had already become quite close to, generously said I could stay at their penthouse on East Seventy-fifth Street for a few weeks before I moved on. I went to the Broadway Theatre to see *The Devils*. The Pope was in town and I remember the cries of "Honor the Holy Father—buy your Pope pennant and pin" from the street vendors. The fact that I can remember that cry more than the production is not a good sign. I spoke with Michael Cacoyannis and, in my gracious manner, told him that I did not agree with what he had done with the play, and I would play those two weeks only if I could do it my way. The play's memorable protagonists, Jeanne and Grandier, meet only at the end of the play, so I needed only to disturb the convent. He agreed totally, but I guess forgot to tell the stage manager, Jean Barrere, who then greeted me with "Okay, honey, let's go over the moves."

"Not so, Mr. Barrere, because they will be totally different moves."

I had one day with him to explain what I was going to do and why. Jean was a sensitive man and bright, but also a disillusioned alcoholic. Somehow he wanted to explore the part with me and was virtually my director. He went to the library and eventually knew more about Jeanne than John Whiting.

As was the case in history, Jeanne was the brilliant daughter of an aristocratic family in Loudun in seventeen-century France. She had been born with curvature of the spine and, because the family was ashamed of her body, it kept her inside the house and never allowed her at table. When she was fourteen she was sent to the convent.

She quickly worked her way up to become the Mother Superior.

The exploits of Grandier, the libertine priest, were gossiped about all through the convent: his affairs with the beautiful women of the town, his delight in great food and wine, and his love of fine laces and materials. His hair was long and black. Jeanne was obsessed by him. She felt sexual longing flood through her for the first time. As Mother Superior, Jeanne invited Grandier to be spiritual advisor to her convent. Grandier declined the offer. As a woman scorned, she announced that Grandier had entered her body in the form of the Devil and incited all those nuns in her charge to feel and say the same thing.

The Church soon heard of this phenomenon and came to Loudun to see the show. And some show it was. A whole convent full of orgiastic nuns. Grandier was interrogated, found guilty of diabolism, stripped of his clothes, whipped, his legs broken and his head shaved with a blunt razor, and thrown at the feet of Jeanne, who, looking at him for the first time, says, "They always spoke of your beauty. Now I see it with my own eyes and I know it to be true."

I had never known anyone with curvature of the spine but Jessica had gone to school with a little girl who was afflicted, and she showed me how she walked and tried to run. Because of the weight of her bent spine she tired easily and had to rest her hand and weight on her knee often.

I always walked across town to the theatre from East Seventy-fifth Street, passing en route many shop windows and people. I would walk one block with curvature of the spine and one block upright. The reflection in the windows was the thing that hurt me the most. Manhattan in the 1960s proved no different: people's reactions were the same as those in the small towns in Victoria for Barry Humphries's spastic—pity, sorrow, or just avert your eyes and move on. By the time I got to the theatre, I hardly needed the hump I had the wardrobe make for my back.

As could be expected, the rehearsal broke into two camps: the loyal Anne Bancroft nuns and the Zoe Caldwell nuns, who were excited by what I was doing.

But I was the Mother Superior and, with Jean Barrere, I succeeded in making Jeanne live. I don't have to play her again either. Of course, the audience was disappointed— they had come to see Anne Bancroft but not many left and those who stayed stood and cheered at the end.

Hume and Jess didn't manage to see *The Devils*. They had left for Africa with Robert Whitehead, whom they had invited to go on safari, and they sweetly said I could remain in the penthouse. This was important, because I was starting another new job. Alan Schneider, the director, knew more about theatre in America and what actors were doing, whether on Broadway, in the regional theatres, summer stock, Off-Broadway, or Off-Off-Broadway, than anyone else. You would find Alan in theatre lobbies all over the country. Casting agents should have had one phone number, Alan's.

He had come backstage during my two weeks of *The Devils* to ask me if I would meet with Tennessee Williams. Alan was to direct his new work on Broadway: two one-act plays, *The Mutilated* and *The Gnädiges Fräulein* under the heading *Slapstick Tragedy*. Alan wanted me to play a gossip columnist in the second play but Tennessee didn't know who I was. I knew who he was. We met, but Tennessee felt very doubtful, and I don't know what Alan said to convince him but I was offered the part. There was nothing in the way I looked or spoke to connect me to the part.

Tennessee was going through a very dark time of rejection by the critics, which seems to be the fate of most great American playwrights just before they are "rediscovered." Had these plays been written by an unknown playwright, and had they opened Off-Broadway, there would have been much rejoicing. "At last, a new, brilliant playwright of black comedy," the banners would have read. But this was old Tennessee Williams, writing surreal nonsense.

The opening play was set in New Orleans. In *The Mutilated*, two ladies of the night, Celeste, a plump little pigeon with breasts she is both proud of and displays, and Trinkit, who is mutilated by a mastectomy, try to survive a brutal world. Tennessee's constant theme—and most great playwrights have a theme that embodies their life—is the brutalization of the frail by the strong. Tennessee's misfit is usually feminine, whether by gender or sensibilities, and always we sit in the theatre and weep, unable to help. The unique thing about these two plays, however, is that Tennessee uses black comedy, for we sit in the audience and laugh as well as cry. It was, I think, Tennessee's way of mocking his own pain. The critics, however, were telling him he no longer had the poetic force to transcend our normal understanding.

I will never forget the Christmas carol he has the carolers sing outside the Silver Dollar Hotel:

I think the strange, the crazed, the queer
Will have their holiday this year
And for a while, a little while,
There will be pity for the wild
A miracle! A miracle!
A sanctuary for the wild.

Margaret Leighton and Kate Reid, two remarkable actresses, played the lost women, while Ming Cho Lee was the set designer and Noel Taylor did the clothes.

We rehearsed in the dreadfully dilapidated Miss Havisham–like atmosphere of the New Amsterdam roof. It was a good rehearsal space for there was a stage and an auditorium. A theatre, in fact. Too often nowadays we rehearse in pristine conditions, but in large wooden-floored rooms with too much daylight. Darkness and a few electric lights are comforting for finding a character.

I can really talk only about *The Gnädiges Fräulein* because that was the play I was absorbed in. It was set in the Florida Keys with one little gray clapboard house blown at a slant by gulf winds. It was a house for transients, with two gray, weathered rocking chairs on the verandah. The keeper of the house was Molly (Kate) and the gossip columnist, Polly (me).

We both wore clown white makeup, clown wigs, and clown shoes. My entrance, which started the play, required me to do five pratfalls to escape the diving cocaloony birds. I went to clown school to learn to pratfall. The accent I picked up from a very well dressed woman in the elevator on the way up to the Cronyns' penthouse, who, while talking of fish, allowed vowels two syllables, sometimes three (fieeush). Once Polly arrived and was seated on a rocking chair, she took out a pad and pencil and a stash of pot and proceeded to roll and smoke Mary Janes. I had learned to roll my own cigarettes when I was on my bush adventure and saw that joints looked the same as my handmade killers, so I didn't think I needed to go to marijuana school. Soon Molly joined me in the other rocking chair and got high too. We rocked in unison and out of unison to the point of falling out of our chairs or standing on our chairs to get a better view of the occupants of Molly's house. This was all orchestrated by Tennessee but we never left the chairs. Then in harmony we would chant, "Huff, huff, huff, *wheee!*"

The most important person in the second play was the Fräulein. She had been an opera singer who had fallen in love with a seal trainer and had learned to balance on top of a big rubber ball and clap her hands like flippers, open her mouth, and compete with the seals for the fish thrown by the trainer. Eventually she became too frail to balance on the ball and was kicked out of the act. Like a lot of frail, frightened people, she ended up in Key West. I hasten to add that the Key West of thirty-five or forty years ago was not the sparkling Key West of today. There was still the naval base and a lot of young sailors with tight bums. One such sailor was in our transient house. There were a lot of hippies in Key West who, in our play, were represented by Indian Joe, a white guy in full Indian regalia.

The cocaloony birds, which had attacked Polly when she arrived, were the same birds with whom the Fräulein was competing for fish down at the docks. They had already taken out one of her eyes, and by the end of the play, they had plucked out the other, so she was blind. I cannot imagine the Fräulein played by anyone other than Maggie Leighton. She was very tall, very thin and frail, and looked like moonlight.

She was also the most heavenly actress. As Polly, I had to be very cruel to her, but each night I wept for her. Not for Maggie, who was so in love with Michael Wilding, and he with her; they had just married. Michael was wickedly funny and Maggie enchantingly funny. They each had a pretty rough passage getting to the other and I always thought of them as two stately galleons who were now in safe harbor.

There were just two problems. Kate could not take a lunch break without three martinis, so afternoon rehearsals were lost, and Alan Schneider insisted that Molly and Polly run all around the house.

"But, Alan, it says in the script we remain in our chairs."

"It will be funnier if you run around."

"Look, Alan, we are only ten days into rehearsal," I said. "I will never leave my chair so I suggest you get some actress who will. I am not cross. I am very grateful and I am out of here."

It was no use appealing to Tennessee. His truth was in the words, not in the slightly confused man who dropped in on rehearsals every day.

Alan rang to ask what would make me come back. "The assurance that I will do only what Williams has written." And a very big Alan Schneider said okay.

Whenever I feel there are things I can do nothing about, I write doggerel or a song. And to the tune of "Trees" I wrote,

> *I doubt that audiences will see*
> *This second play by Tennessee.*
> *A play that's fraught with homely birds,*
> *If only Kate could learn the words.*
> *They'll not hear our, "Huff, huff, wheee,*
> *We are so sorry, Tennessee.*

The play lasted two weeks and yet I won my first Tony—not because I was brilliant but because Tennessee was.

Three years later, in 1969, I went to Key West and

there were the little gray clapboard houses blown at a slant by the gulf winds with two weathered rocking chairs on the verandah. There were the pelicans down at the dock competing for fish. There were the hippies dressed as Indians, and the sailors still had those tight bums. And inside the bars, there were quite a few leftover ladies with dyed hair, red lips, bright eye shadow, and shoes that belonged to another time or someone else—and, because of the heat, a lot of white powder was caked on their faces. Sad clowns.

I realized that, like all great artists, Tennessee didn't write lies. He wrote the truth as seen through his eyes, and he enriched our knowledge and understanding. Artists make us stop and look.

I still had a month to fill in before my next job so I arranged a huge party for Jess and Hume at their apartment. I had it catered by William Poll of Lexington Avenue and with the help of Hume's secretary, Sylvia Brooks; Wilhelmena Reavis, Jessica's theatre maid; and Malcolm Wells, Hume's theatre man. I invited, by phone, everyone in New York whom I thought the Cronyns would like to see and who would like to see the Cronyns home safe from Africa. I had to tell Jess and Hume that there was to be a party because this was their penthouse, but they were not given a guest list. They had only been home two days. I asked them to go to bed for the afternoon as it might be a long night. And it was.

The party started at six on a Saturday and lasted until six on Sunday morning. That meant that friends who were in a show could come before or after or both and the same for people who were seeing a show. For those with true stamina, they could stay the whole twelve hours.

The party was a great success. Jess and Hume looked rested and tan and took their place by the elevator and were surprised and very happy to see so many friends. They also stayed the twelve hours. It was the least I could do, for they had allowed me to stay for five months, rent free. They were fast becoming family.

When Robert Whitehead, who had missed the party, arrived from London, where he had been coproducing *The Prime of Miss Jean Brodie* with Vanessa Redgrave as Brodie, Jess and Hume invited him to dinner and we did the dishes again, again to no avail. The Cronyns finally gave up on the matchmaking.

Perversely, of our own accord, we then fell in love. But I had to leave New York and Robert because my next job was at the Shaw Festival in Niagara-on-the-Lake, which was then held in the town hall with sheets strung down the middle of the one dressing room backstage. One side for women, one side for men. It was good work, good actors, and good plays. I played Orinthia in *The Apple Cart* again and was no better than before but my Lina Szczepanowska, the aviatrix, in *Misalliance* was very good.

I had a phone put in my rather drab motel room at Robert's suggestion and spent all my wages on nightly phone calls to Robert. His phone bills were larger than mine but I thought he could handle it.

When the festival ended Robert drove to Niagara-on-the-Lake and led the way, in his Mustang convertible, to his beautiful little eighteenth-century fieldstone farm-house in Bucks County, Pennsylvania. I followed in my old Corvair Monza. I was now Robert's woman. I also, one day, would become his wife.

He had rented a large two-room apartment, filled with light, at 3 East Sixty-sixth Street, on the ninth floor (I knew we'd be okay, because three is my lucky number). It was painted flat white and had full transparent white curtains to the floor and a king-size bed. Robert's friends were all happy that he was happy, but of course didn't think it would last. Neither did I, because there were great slices of the day when he would cut off and go into himself. I should have understood the act of mourning is not a quick act.

Meanwhile, Robert's close friends were sweetly welcoming—with the exception of Maureen Stapleton, a truly great actress, who thought I was a truly ambitious actress who would use Robert and leave him. Little did she know. She does now and has become a truly great friend.

Throughout my career I have had enormous good luck and I worked very hard, but taking the next job could hardly be called ambitiously planning a career. What I didn't realize was that Robert was that year's catch. Why not? He was a very handsome, successful widower. What others didn't realize was that his eligible status meant nothing to me. I just knew it was great being with him and he made wonderful love. The good thing was that neither of us needed the other for work.

～ 20 ～

I Will Be Cleopatra

I HAD BEEN asked by Michael Langham to return to Stratford, Ontario, to play Lady Anne to Alan Bates's Richard III, Mistress Page in *The Merry Wives of Windsor*, and Cleopatra opposite Christopher Plummer's Antony.

I asked Michael whether Tanya would be designing *Antony and Cleopatra*.

"Of course. Who else?"

Tanya is the daughter of Benno Moiseiwitsch, a world-renowned Russian pianist, and Daisy Kennedy, a captivating Australian violinist, who later married John Drinkwater, the English playwright and poet. Tanya took from both parents, but was her totally original self.

"Then is it possible for me to meet with her and talk? She is so calm and wise and will set me on the right road to study and learn all I need to know about Shakespeare's greatest role for a woman."

We met in New York and went straight to the Metropolitan Museum of Art to spend most of the day in Egypt. The Met's collection is massive and magnificent, and I learned that Cleopatra was born in 69 B.C. and died when she was thirty-nine. She was part of the Ptolemy dynasty that had ruled Egypt from the time of the death of Alexander the Great, of Macedonia. She became queen of Egypt in 51 B.C. at the age of eighteen. Her ten-year-old brother, Ptolemy XIII, became her co-ruler and, in compliance with Egyptian tradition, her husband. While we were at the museum we decided to round out the day with the Greeks, for Cleopatra too had taken from both sides of her ancestors.

The next day we went to the wig maker, a talented older man whom I had never seen before or since, and talked extensively about the color and shape of Cleopatra's hair, Tanya making sure that what was right for Cleopatra would also be right for me.

Because of the heat and the sand and the fleas, Egyptian bodies were denuded of all hair—except the great people, who could be bathed and perfumed by their handmaidens. It is said that Cleopatra had her pubic hair straightened, hennaed, and oiled, and that it was encouraged to grow as long as it could. The floors of her palace were shined so they could mirror this hidden beauty. I wondered if I should order a long silky merkin.

Tanya and I said good-bye and went our own ways, she to Stratford to design and oversee the making of the clothes and me to the Bahamas. Robert and I flew to Nassau to meet up with Hume and Jess and spend two days making sure we had the right provisions for a boat that Hume had chartered to take us through the wondrous world of the Exuma Keys.

Hume had been coming to the Bahamas since he was in knee socks and knew, like a native Bahamian, the waters and reefs and all the creatures living in them. He virtually swam like them. He knew the joys and the dangers and they seemed to realize that he knew. Jessica and he had developed an island, Children's Bay Cay, and lived there on and off for fifteen years. It wasn't merely the sea creatures under the water who admired and respected the Cronyns, but all the people who lived on land did as well.

The real revelation was Jess—beautiful, ladylike, gentle Jess was a fearless killer as soon as she put on her wet suit. I had been brought up in Australia, the home of the great white shark, where swimmers swam within the confines of steel netting. I said, "Sharks, barracudas . . . are you mad to ask me to drop off the side of a whaler into unknown waters?" But because of the fearlessness of my fellow travelers, I too lost my fear—not all of it, but enough to join in.

When eventually I told my dad that I had swum with barracuda and sharks, he said, "You do what you like, Zoe. As for me, I don't go down there and trouble them. They don't come up here and trouble me."

We had a really good Bahamian captain of Welsh descent who was white and a beautiful young ship's mate who was black. He dove, without gear, to the depth of seventy-five feet and brought up wonders for us to examine and sometimes to eat. We ate a lot of seafood, locally grown fruit and vegetables, and rice, and we swam. I became brown as a berry—not Jess; she was too savvy about the sun. The men looked like ancient Greek sailors. I mean, like the sailors of ancient Greece.

The weather was glorious, the sand white powder, and the water . . . well, the water of the Caribbean was and still is like no other water in the world.

I discovered shells and became a collector. There was nothing scientific about it—I just took the shells back to the boat to clean and wonder at the imagination and variety of nature. They would have been ground into sand so I don't think I became a major environmental risk. But the real stab to my stomach would come from seeing, down the beach, a piece of glass shining in the sun, because it might possibly be a Portuguese glass fishing ball. Portuguese fishermen wove these glass balls into the edge of their nets, to let them see where in the water the nets were. Somehow some cut loose and floated all the way to the Exumas. They were exquisite. Like jewels, they were the most delicate shades of blue, gray, green, and amethyst, and I found them. Whatever beach we stopped at, I found a ball. Beginner's luck. And because I thought that they would always be there, I gave most of them away. But the very next year they were gone, and in their place were nasty, orange, plastic, hard balls with two rings at the top like ears to secure them to the nets. And tarred all over. Tar had begun to dirty up those pristine beaches.

When you become pregnant you consciously take care of your body for the baby. Taking on a role is very similar. All through the Bahamas, I was making my body fit and my mind relaxed for Cleopatra. When you accept a role, whatever the role, everything is grist for the mill. I had no waking moment without her. This behavior is not attractive because you become an avaricious seeker of knowledge. Since there were not a lot of people walking around the Bahamas or New York who had actually known Cleopatra, I had to go to Plutarch. I knew that Plutarch and Holinshed had been Shakespeare's great sources, so why not mine? Off I went to Canada with Plutarch under one arm for the ancient Romans and Holinshed under the other for Anne and the ancient Brits. I thought Mum could be my source for Mistress Page and I was right.

I knew that somehow this season would become the cornerstone for the rest of my life, both professionally and privately.

The company was its old splendid self. Alan Bates was *the* new man. We were all a bit anxious about this glamorous, good-looking film star. Would he think himself the cat's pajamas and would we have to bring him down a peg or two? He had been a stage actor so maybe he would be fine. In fact, he was more than fine. He was a marvelous, humorous fellow, and as soon as he and I met I felt that I had known him a long while, but that there was no danger of romance.

John Hirsch was to direct *Richard III* and Desmond Heeley design. The cast was, as always, strong and the women exceptional. The boar was Richard's emblem, and when women spoke to him or of him, the words they used were dog, bottled spider, foul toad, hedgehog. He was hideously misshapen but I have known sweet, gentle, bright misshapen people. I believe the health of a person, a town, a country, is possible only when there is an easy access to both masculine and feminine sensibilities. Both are needed, at different times, whatever one's gender, but if there is a permanent excess of one or the other, the person, the town, the country, the world, is out of kilter. Richard III had not been the recipient of feminine sensibilities, starting with his mother, so I don't think he even knew of their existence. He was bright beyond measure and could charm and fascinate, but all his involvement with fellow humans was harsh, hurtful, and murderous. This affected the whole country during his reign in the later years of the fifteenth century. No one was safe and no one trusted anyone.

"Set down, set down your honorable load," the first words of Lady Anne, rang in my ears because the most exquisite Anne, young, vulnerable and pure, in the person of Vivien Leigh, had spoken them at the Princess Theatre in Melbourne, in 1948, and I assumed that pure, high English sound was right. I no longer believe that. Anne was fifteen, already widowed, and in deep mourning for her father-in-law, King Henry VI. She had just walked behind the corpse of her husband. It was a short marriage. Her time with Edward, Prince of Wales, was brought to a halt by his death at Richard's hands, and before she had time to think of changing her black widow's weeds, she had to take an even longer veil of black to walk behind the corpse of Edward's father. Pall-bearing men, halberd-bearing men, and corpses. Lady Anne—this is not only your life but will be forever and ever. Suddenly the killer himself appears and all the venom, passion, pain, and sexual fury can be spewed out. It must have been spectacularly thrilling for Richard too: a young, hot, female teenager and he hurling verbal insults across a bleeding corpse. Usually the female sex averted its eyes. Gradually it becomes a seduction and almost a rape and the audience should understand this young girl's reaction. Spider is an apt name for Richard and he has lured her to his web. This meeting is not mentioned in Holinshed but Shakespeare knew you had to get the attention of the groundlings quickly.

Desmond Heeley's sketches were a great help. I had one black gown, with veil, and one white, with headdress, both enabling me to be fifteen, whereas I was in fact thirty-three.

Poor little Anne lived such a short life. She had thrown a curse at whomever became Richard's wife, never realizing she would be the one to catch it.

Alan was a remarkable Richard. He was crooked where he should have been and withered where he should have been, and evil, but very bright and seductive.

Alan had taken a house outside of Stratford for his privacy. I found my own house half an hour from town, in St. Mary's, and drove my yellow jeep with its red canopy through the early morning to the theatre and back at night. St. Mary's was perfect; so was the little house with an acre of grass down to a stream. Robert flew into Toronto every Friday in his chinos, white shirt, and navy blazer and flew out Monday morning.

I remember the first time Robert set foot in that house. I was deep into Ravi Shankar, it being the late 1960s. He stopped at the door and said, "What is that?"

I answered gently, as if to a child, "Oh, darling, that is Indian music played by Ravi Shankar on a sitar."

"I know that, but is it a morning or afternoon rhythm?"

How was I to know he had spent six months in India after the end of World War II?

The Merry Wives of Windsor seems to work well, whoever does it and even when it's sung. David Williams directed and I played Mum. I rang home to tell Mum that she had been a great success as Mistress Page. She couldn't wait to tell me that she had won the first prize in an essay competition in Melbourne and that Dad had had a great success as himself. The title of her essay was "The Model Husband," and when Mum received her award the mayor asked whether the model husband would like to speak. Dad came to the microphone and said he was proud of his wife and her award, but just before leaving home, he had checked the word *model* in the dictionary and found it meant a small edition of the real thing.

Rehearsals began for *Antony and Cleopatra*, but Christopher Plummer was delayed in Greece filming *Oedipus the King* with Lilli Palmer, and we were forced to start without him. I was a great fan of Chris but had met him only twice, briefly. The first time was after a performance of *The Devils*. I had invited Wilhelmena Reavis, Jessica Tandy's and Lynn Fontanne's theatre maid, to be my guest at the performance, and afterward we would go to dinner. There was a knock at the door, which I opened and there were two men wearing dark fedoras and overcoats. Thoughts of Mafia floated through my mind until one, whom I recognized as Jason Robards, introduced the other as Christopher Plummer and asked could I join them for dinner or at least some drinks. "Oh, I'm sorry, I can't come because I'm having dinner with Willie." And they left. Jason later told me they thought "Willie" was some hunk in the dressing room, never dreaming it might be a tiny, elegant, theatre maid.

Very soon thereafter, I went backstage to congratulate Chris on his stunning performance as Pizarro in *The Royal Hunt of the Sun.* I was sweating in embarrassment and he was sweating from his performance, so it was a pretty quick handshake. But the mystery of the fedoras the night of Willie became clear. Chris took off his wig, revealing a shaved head, and of course Jason had shaved his head for Grandier. And it was New York and winter.

Michael Langham's ability to direct Shakespeare is wondrous to behold. All those endless battles with the need to know whose side you are on are, in Michael's hands, kindergarten stuff. Other directors have this skill but Michael also reads and understands the text with all its subtleties. I would never have become the Cleopatra I did become without his gentle guidance. Masculine and feminine sensibilities are readily available to him, as they should be for all directors.

Meanwhile, there was a lot of talk about how dare Chris put me in the position of beginning this great love story with one lover absent. I didn't mind. I had the most marvelous court around me on the Nile. Charmian, Cleopatra's attendant, was the kind of woman I hope Cleopatra had had. There were no secrets and she watched me like a hawk. To ease me, pleasure me, and protect me. Her name, in this life, was Dawn Greenhalgh and I could not have played Cleopatra without her. Cleopatra's court was relaxed and playful, and allowed great intimacy because she was so sure and easy in her authority. An actor should never "play" a king or queen. It is the world around them on stage that tells an audience they are royal.

The unexpected windfall of Chris arriving later than expected was that I had the time to read, side by side, Plutarch's *Life of Marcus Antonius* and Shakespeare's *Antony and Cleopatra*.

I learned that, historically, Cleopatra was not beautiful. There is a lot of discussion about her nose and her very heavy breasts. But she was a quick-witted, highly educated Greek descendant skilled in mathematics, politics, and business. She also was the only Ptolemy who spoke Egyptian. "It was a pleasure merely to hear the sound of her voice" wrote Plutarch, "with which like an instrument with many strings, she could pass from one language to another; so that there were few of the barbarian nations that she answered by an interpreter; to most of them she spoke herself, as to the Ethiopians, Troglodytes, Hebrews, Arabians, Syrians, Medes, Parthians and many others whose language she had learned." Leaders coming from Rome to meet this woman, who had held in her sway two of the greatest leaders of the western world, were shocked to see her because she did not match the image of a gorgeous empress they'd envisioned. Nonetheless, after spending time with her they went back to Rome and described her as the most beautiful woman in the world. Shakespeare has Antony's friend, Enobarbus describe her best:

> *I saw her once*
> *Hop forty paces through the public street;*
> *and having lost her breath, she spoke, and panted,*
> *That she did make defect perfection,*
> *and, breathless, pow'r breathe forth.*
>
> . . . .
>
> *Age cannot wither her, nor custom stale*
> *Her infinite variety: other women cloy*
> *The appetites they feed, but she makes hungry*
> *Where most she satisfies; for vilest things*
> *Become themselves in her, that the holy priests*
> *Bless her when she is riggish [lewd].*

The Enobarbus of William Hutt was relaxed, cynical, and superior, everything the character was meant to be.

I went every day to the costume department to watch

our world evolve. I took the word *tawny* for the color of her skin and concocted a makeup for my whole body using oils and perfume. The soles of my feet and the palms of my hands would be hennaed, but not permanently (it was repertory and I knew that real henna was long-lasting, so a makeup that would stay and then be removed became a challenge).

Years later, in Morocco, I asked the ladies at a wedding to henna my hands. They made a sweet-smelling pad of what looked like grass and spread it on my palms. I then stood in the sun for one hour with my palms up and my fingers stretched out. Then they washed off the pad and I had bright red hands that smelled musky and foreign. Three weeks later I cooked our Thanksgiving dinner with pale red hands that still smelled musky and foreign.

Besides poring over the costumes, I had brought with me blowups of Egyptian kings, queens, goddesses, temples, and friezes from a book on Egypt's architecture, sculpture, and paintings that I had obtained from the Cairo Museum. I also found some wonderful colored prints of the Ajanta Caves of Maharashtra in India in a little stationery store in Stratford. Every inch of that little St. Mary's house was covered with foreign and erotic images. Not fully satisfied, I perfumed the house with musky foreign scents so that my only escape from Cleopatra was to rush to the theatre and become Lady Anne or Mistress Page. I was becoming consumed with Cleopatra, and now needed Chris to arrive. And he did.

He strode into the theatre, tanned, gorgeous, and dressed all in white, and walked straight to me and took possession. I knew how Cleopatra must have felt. Now, it was a known fact that Chris took possession of all his leading ladies in more ways than one. The company couldn't wait for Robert to arrive. Robert and Christopher were both from Montreal, and Robert had known Chris since he was a schoolboy. They were almost related, but I was Robert's woman.

However, there was a slight buzz in the theatre the night they sat together to watch *The Merry Wives of Windsor*. Then word came backstage that the two Montrealers were taking off their trousers in the VIP room. What! What was going on in the VIP room? Jackets I would understand, but trousers? At last all was revealed— of the problem, not the men. The Queen, the real queen, Elizabeth II, was in Ottawa to dedicate the National Arts Centre of Canada and Christopher was supposed to fly up to make a speech of welcome. He decided he could not miss one more day of rehearsal, so he asked Robert to stand in for him.

"Oh sure," said Robert, "but in chinos, a white shirt, and navy blue blazer?"

"Wear my clothes and take my speech."

"You and I are different shapes and the trousers won't fit."

"Let's try."

They fit, and we all lived happily ever after. I commemorated the occasion as follows:

Robert Ward Whitehead
Where have you been?
Been up to Ottawa,
Spoke with the Queen.
Robert Ward Whitehead
What did you wear?
Chris Plummer's suit,
But I wore my own hair.

I knew playing with Chris would be a good experience but I wasn't prepared for it to be so easy and natural. He filled the male role so totally that all I had to do was fill the female. If an actor doesn't take up the male oxygen, I tend to move in to keep the audience awake and in its seats. Bad for the actor, bad for the play, and bad for me.

The genius of Shakespeare is that Cleopatra is a composite of all women and in all aspects.

Because Christopher was so bold and unafraid and led me to be the same, we built a relationship onstage of absolute freedom to love, to play, to fight. We were royal, we were carnal, we were leaders, we were slaves, and anything was possible. We were young, we were old, and so intimate that not even death would part us. That is the tragedy of Antony and Cleopatra. They are neither wholly great nor wholly corrupt, but like many great leaders they are bold, fearless, craven, and stupid, and when their world is destroyed our world is vastly diminished. The tragedy is not theirs but ours.

Cleopatra, at eighteen, had found a powerful man, thirty-three years her elder, for whom she had genuine respect, whose intelligence and wit matched her own. His name was Julius Caesar. It was a union of two great, ambitious rulers. Caesar's ambition was for Rome and Cleopatra's for a revival of Egypt as a world power. They had a son, Caesarion, and the Queen of Egypt wanted that son to be the ruler of both countries, thus the ruler of the world. That was her great overriding ambition and it eventually brought about her downfall and the end of the Ptolemy dynasty. Caesar asked Cleopatra to bring

Caesarion, whom he acknowledged as his son, to Rome, but the Ides of March were upon them and Caesar was murdered by his own friends.

Cleopatra fled back to Alexandria, had her brother Ptolemy XIV murdered, and placed four-year-old Caesarion on the throne beside her. She had watched Mark Antony while in Rome and decided Marcus Antonius, about a dozen years older than she, would be her Roman power. Each wanted something from the other. The wealth of the Ptolemys was legendary, and Antony needed it to fight his battles against Octavian Caesar and other ambitious Romans. He invited her to dine with him in Tarsus.

Cleopatra knew about his limited strategic and tactical abilities, his blue blood, his drinking, his womanizing, his vulgarity, and his ambition. She put on a show for Antony. As Plutarch writes, "She sailed in a gilded barge with out spread sails of purple, while oars of silver beat time to the music of flutes, fifes, and harps. She herself lay all along under a canopy of cloth of gold dressed as Venus and beautiful young boys like painted cupids stood on each side to fan her. Her maids were dressed as sea nymphs, some steering at the rudder, some working at the ropes. The perfumes diffused themselves from the vessel to the shore which was covered with multitudes, part following the galley up the river on either bank or running out of the city to see the sight." It was a calculated display to attract the attention of a vulgar man.

As Plutarch tells us, Cleopatra and Mark Antony spent the winter of 41–40 B.C. in Alexandria. She never left his side and matched him in every way. She would play dice with him, drink and swear with him, follow him in any bodily activity, and make bawdy love with him. Marcus Antonius was used to Roman matrons and glorious whores, and here was a blue-blooded Ptolemy woman who was capable of everything. She never let him out of her sight. Over the course of their love she also bore him three children, the twins Alexander Helios and Cleopatra Selene and then Ptolemy Philadelphos.

And this is where Shakespeare's play begins.

The historical facts astound you but you realize the necessity of a great playwright to make the story of these two legendary figures transcend the facts. That is what playwrights do, and they do it in the slyest way. Just as you feel empathy for the characters, they confound you by doing something so dumb, so hurtful, to themselves and others, that your emotion turns to rage. Then just as you are sure you have no sympathy, their frailty is revealed and you weep. Christopher Plummer is an actor who is not afraid to show his frailty. Our scenes together seemed inevitable, and I held nothing back.

And here, I have chosen to end my journey toward being an actress for several reasons. In first preparing to be and then playing Cleopatra, I was forced to take on a deeper involvement than I had ever had with a part. I gave all of myself to her, which is a dangerous thing to do in theatre or in life. When the play closes or the loved one leaves, where are you if you have given all of yourself? Who are you? It takes me usually six months to regain my self, my life. That takes its toll. Cleopatra was the first woman to demand that of me and she brought me to another depth of acting. Not everyone wants that depth from me but that is what I must do.

When we were nearing the end of our 1967 season, playing a lot of matinées for schools, I was asked by the stage manager, who was relaying the company manager's request, to cover my breasts with a piece of material, because of the presence of schoolchildren. "And will Chris and I play differently?" Of course, I refused to tone down the performance or use the piece of material.

I felt the kids were bright enough to sense our distrust of them if we had altered the production. I was right. They listened and laughed like an Elizabethan audience, except for one group, one afternoon. They had behaved rudely and I longed to tell them so. Suddenly with the asp at my breast, I blew. I stood up, walked to the front of the stage and told them how rude they were. I told them about the piece of material that I had rejected because of my belief in them. I told them I was very, very tired and had to play Mistress Page that night. I gave them a choice. We could stop the play right here or we could continue to the end, but the choice was theirs. They must tell me what they wanted. Nobody made a peep.

"Speak up and tell me right now."

A little voice said, "Please continue, Cleopatra." And the theatre was suddenly full of young voices. "Please continue, please continue, please continue." Easy for them to say. We were all of us so charged that I had no idea how to continue. Then Charmian said, "Dissolve, thick cloud, and rain, that I may say the gods themselves do weep." And we were back.

Of course they stood and cheered at curtain, because they were alive and we were alive. We now live in a highly technological world where a lot of people experience life through machines. But when communication is still made directly by living people standing in front of other living people, the result is dangerous because anything can happen.

I especially like one scene between Antony and Cleopatra because it could be played in any house. Antony has flown into an Othello-like fit of jealousy upon seeing a messenger from Caesar kiss Cleopatra's hand, and it takes his lady quite a while to calm him. At last, he says, "Come, let's have one more gaudy night . . . , fill our bowls; once more let's mock the midnight bell."

Cleopatra became for me the cornerstone of my career, because I knew that all the women I had played, all the women I had known and reacted to, and, for that matter, all the men went into my being able to answer Antony by saying:

> *It is my birthday.*
> *I had thought to have held it poor; but since my lord*
> *Is Antony again, I will be Cleopatra.*

And I was.

Born in Melbourne, Australia, at the onset of the Great Depression, Zoe Caldwell began her professional acting career as Slightly Soiled in *Peter Pan* at the age of nine. Caldwell became a tried and true professional at the age of fourteen, performing frequently on the radio. At the age of twenty-four, she went to Stratford-upon-Avon where she began a Shakespearean career that would culminate ten years later in Canada with her portrayal of Cleopatra, the Bard's greatest female role. She has since traveled most of the English-speaking world, performing Chekhov, Brecht, Williams, and Pinter, among many others, and has expanded her career to include directing and teaching. Caldwell has won virtually every prestigious award in theater, including four Tony Awards for her leading roles in *Slapstick Tragedy*, *The Prime of Miss Jean Brodie*, *Medea*, and *Master Class*. In 1970, the Queen of England awarded her the Order of the British Empire. She currently resides in New York, with her husband, Robert Whitehead, with whom she has two sons.

I Will Be Cleopatra forms the basis of three public lectures that Caldwell gave at The New York Public Library in October 2001.